Wanting

What

You

Have

A Self-Discovery Workbook

Timothy Miller, Ph.D.

NEW HARBINGER PUBLICATIONS

Distributed in the U.S.A. by Publishers Group West; in Canada by Raincoast
Books; in Great Britain by Airlift Book Company, Ltd.; in South Africa by
Real Books, Ltd.; in Australia by Boobook; and in New Zealand by Tandem
Press.

"Strange Wine," from *Amazing Stories*, 5th edition, by Harlan Ellison (New
York: HarperCollins, 1976).

Cover design by Poulson/Gluck Design
Text design by Tracy Marie Powell

ISBN 1-57224-153-5 Paperback

New Harbinger Publication's Website address: www.newharbinger.com

First Printing

菜の花や
月は東に日は西に

蕪村

Contents

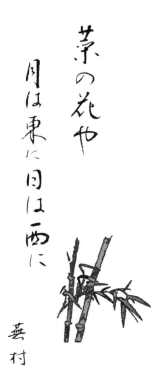

菜の花や
月は東に日は西に

蕪村

A Few Small,
Important Matters

Previewers

Many of the exercises in this book have been test-driven by volunteer previewers. Some of these people subscribe to my automated e-mail list (turn to page 207 for more information). In order to protect previewer privacy, I have used pseudonyms or used composites of two or more previewer reactions.

Gender

Wishing to avoid both awkward syntax and sexist language, I have alternated genders in passages that require gendered pronouns like "he" or "she," "him" or "her." I have tried to do so without regard to traditional sex roles. Consequently, in these pages, you may find female coaches and male nurses, and good and bad people of both sexes.

Workbooks

Libraries are one of our most precious cultural institutions, and workbooks cause librarians headaches. If you check this workbook out of a library, please *photocopy* the exercises you want to do. In that way you will not spoil the original for other borrowers. Actually, I recommend photocopying even if this book is your own because you might want to repeat some of the exercises many times.

Capitalization

As a sign of reverence, I usually capitalize the terms "Compassion," "Attention," and "Gratitude." Although my religious beliefs are somewhat abstract and often in flux, Compassion, Attention, and Gratitude are three things I have felt able to believe in for many years.

Additionally, capitalizing these words signifies that I use these terms in a specialized way, as I will discuss in the opening chapters. I avoid capitalizing related words such as "compassionate" or "ungrateful" because this practice would generate a forest of distracting and possibly pretentious capital letters.

菜の花や
月は東に
日は西に

蕪村

Introduction

Since the beginning of recorded history, wise people from all parts of the world have said in one way or another that the secret to happiness is not to get what you want, but to want what you have. You can find variations of this idea in classical Greek philosophy, in Native American and Native Australian religion, in Buddhism, Christianity, Islam and Judaism, in modern fiction, poetry, and commentary. One well-known source of this idea is Henry David Thoreau, who wrote, "That man is richest whose pleasures are cheapest." Another is the Talmud, where it is written, "Who is rich? He who is pleased with his portion."

Like any other broad and powerful idea, wanting what you have is easily misunderstood and misapplied. Many people leap to the unfortunate conclusion that wanting what you have means giving up ambition or personal responsibility in favor of some passive, blissful state. Nothing could be further from the truth.

Happy, contented people work for the love of their work, whether they are celebrities or custodians; they run for the love of the race. Happy, contented people are responsible spouses, parents, and citizens; they do the right thing because they love to do the right thing. The people most likely to harm the earth and its people are those who crave wealth and power for their own sake and don't care how they get them.

Some people tell me that they already want what they have. Perhaps these people are unusually contented and compassionate. Some people are indeed born with calm and cheerful dispositions. Other people may have learned about wanting what they have in church, psychotherapy, or spiritual practice. Nevertheless, people who think they have already learned to want what they have have missed the point.

Wanting what you have is a process, not a destination. Saying "I already want what I have" is like saying "I am already wise" or "I am already musical." Bright people never run out of interesting new things to understand better. Musical people spend their entire lives perfecting their performances and musical knowledge. It is impossible to be perfectly intelligent. It is impossible to be perfectly musical. It is impossible to perfect the art of wanting what you have. As your life unfolds, greed, resentment, despair, and worry will tempt you in ten thousand ways. This is the human situation in every culture and at every time in history.

I recently read a magazine article that reviewed all the technological triumphs we have seen in the twentieth century, from the earliest airplanes to the Internet and the Hubble space telescope. I like gadgets as much as the next person, and I do have scientific inclinations. The article was thrilling, in a way. Yet, upon reflection, I realized that none of these innovations have actually made people happier, more ethical, or more loving. In fact, they may have made people less happy because the number of things a normal person might crave but never possess grows larger every day.

High-tech societies are no happier than low-tech societies. Dazzling technological innovations always produce unintended consequences. If the telephone had never been invented, most people would live close to their relatives, as most people have done since time began. If people still lived close to their relatives, there might be less loneliness and less divorce. If the automobile had never been invented, people would know their neighbors better. There would be less crime. As long as people have the basic necessities of life, prosperity does not increase happiness. Fascinating and convenient gadgets do not increase happiness.

A faster Internet connection might be pretty cool; videophones could be a kick. But these won't change human nature. What humanity needs most desperately is a technology that will help people enjoy the short and uncertain spans of their lives while behaving generously and decently. I searched that magazine article carefully for a single advance of this nature. None was mentioned. Not even the need was mentioned.

In this workbook, and my first book, *How to Want What You Have: Discovering the Magic and Grandeur of Ordinary Existence*, I do my best to introduce a technology of joy and kindness. Mine is not the only technology of joy and kindness. No one can say whether it is the best. Your concern is how well it works for you, and perhaps for the people you love.

You might wonder why I have gone to all the trouble of developing this new combination of theory and method when so many others, more able than me, have already taught so much. This is a fair question.

I have an unusual temperament; sometimes it seems odd even to myself. Some of my friends and family find it very odd indeed, though they are usually polite enough not to say so. My temperament mixes curiosity, idealism, and hedonism with skepticism, tough-mindedness, and high ethical standards. I admire scientific rigor and don't do faith well; I'm not even sure I *want* faith. Accordingly, the personal and spiritual growth books I've read often don't seem quite satisfactory to me. Some seem founded on naive and scientifically suspect beliefs. Some promise the moon. Others ignore urgent concerns about social justice and environmental protection. After many years of frustrations and disappointment, I decided to work out what makes sense to me. *How to Want What You Have* and this workbook are the result.

My personal characteristics will be reflected in what I write and how I write it. This is so for all authors. In some measure, I have written for an audience of people much like me not out of egotism but because this is the only audience I can completely understand. Readers of similar temperament might find themselves at home in these pages. I welcome other readers to take what's good here and combine it as best they can with their own faiths and temperaments.

Personal and spiritual growth need not be mysterious or arduous, in my opinion. If self-improvement was always very difficult, personal and spiritual growth would be rare phenomena and there would be little hope for the human race! Yet many self-improvement methods are so obscure and inconvenient they seem nearly impossible, particularly for people who work forty or more hours per week supporting families.

I have tried to develop a method of personal and spiritual growth not any harder than, say, learning to play tennis or basketball, and not much harder to understand. I've called this method learning to "want what you have."

The requirements for basketball improvement are pretty obvious. You need a clear idea of your goal. You need a simple method for working toward your goal. You also need a strong desire to succeed. Frequent reminders of the benefits of success will sustain your desire to succeed. Your simple method would be practicing the fundamentals of the sport—dribbling, free throws, layups, hook shots, and so on. Your desire to succeed comes from your own personality and life experience. In wanting what you have, your simple method focuses on three fundamentals, or principles, as I call them: the systematic and diligent practice of Compassion, Attention, and Gratitude.

A coach improves your odds of success. That's why every major sports team has at least one coach. A good coach will show you how to use your practice time more effectively and will point out the subtle weaknesses in your game. She will inspire you to do your best and remind you of the rewards of playing well. She may occasionally warn you of the costs of failure. She'll share a few insider's tips you might never have figured out for yourself.

With this workbook, you can work toward wanting what you have. As author of this workbook, I am a kind of coach. My duty to you is to help you master the fundamentals—Compassion, Attention, and Gratitude. I'll show you some possible errors and how to avoid them. I'll show you some hidden opportunities and how to exploit them. I'll try to inspire you from time to time and remind you of the benefits of success and the penalties of failure.

A coach can't do everything, nor can a workbook. If after reading this workbook and doing some of the exercises you are not convinced that wanting what you have is a good idea, or if your desire for success is weak, that is your business. I hope you will at least conclude that I did a fair job of coaching.

菜
の
花
や

月
は
東
に
日
は
西
に

蕪
村

1

Habits of Thought

Wanting what you have is a simple slogan that reflects a deep and challenging goal. The methods I suggest for wanting what you have revolve around three fundamental principles: Compassion, Attention, and Gratitude. I deliberately modeled the practice of Compassion, Attention, and Gratitude after modern methods of cognitive psychotherapy. I did so because cognitive psychotherapy is easier to understand and more widely recognized as effective than any other psychotherapeutic method. Accordingly, it's necessary to describe cognitive psychotherapy before I can describe Compassion, Attention, and Gratitude.

For thousands of years, religious teachers and philosophers have coached, inspired, reminded, and warned people who wished to better themselves. Did these teachers do much good? Pessimists would say the bloodiness and stupidity of human history indicates they failed. Optimists would say while they didn't solve *all* the human race's problems, they made the world more livable. Perhaps they made civilization possible. I deliberately cultivate optimism in myself and encourage my friends and clients to do the same thing, so I'll take the more optimistic view.

In any case, philosophers and religious teachers of old would have been more successful if they had known about modern cognitive methods for psychotherapy and self-help. Until recently, psychotherapeutic change was a murky and mysterious business, and so was spiritual growth. Self-help was often trendy, but its value was widely doubted. Psychotherapy and psychological self-help are so similar to spiritual growth and self-help it is hard to distinguish the two. As you read the following discussion of psychotherapy for a depressed woman named Monica, think about how the nine principles and procedures outlined here could be applied to personal growth.

Twenty-five years of careful scientific research have shown that these nine statements are true for almost anyone:

1. **Many upsetting thoughts and beliefs are simply bad habits**. Many people, including Monica, honestly believe that they are stupid. Monica is ashamed of being stupid and believes her life is and will remain unhappy because she is stupid. Incidents that remind her of her alleged stupidity often cause her pain and sometimes make her unaccountably angry. Monica has average or above-average intelligence. She has a reasonable repertoire of skills and talents. Nevertheless, she honestly believes she is stupid. Her repetitive thoughts about her own stupidity represent nothing more than a bad habit.

2. **Certain thoughts and beliefs can cause serious emotional problems such as depression and anxiety.** As Monica dwells on how stupid she is, she becomes discouraged about her ability to lead a happy, productive life. If her discouragement becomes deep, she will become depressed. Monica's beliefs about her stupidity might grow so strong that she will fear entering situations where she will appear stupid to others. In that case, she has developed an anxiety disorder.

3. **Habits of thought can be critically examined.** Monica could critically examine her beliefs about her stupidity: *Am I good at some things that require intelligence? When I make bad decisions, is the cause stupidity or strong emotions? How well do I read? How is my vocabulary?*

   After this kind of critical examination, Monica might conclude, *Jeez, maybe I'm not so stupid after all. What have I been thinking all these years?*

4. **Habits of thought can be disputed.** Monica might learn to notice the times she repeats her habitual thought about being stupid. Each time the problem thought repeats itself, she might think, for instance, *I got pretty good grades in high school. I read well. I understand current events very well. My spelling and grammar are excellent. How could I be stupid?* Later she can shorten this to *I am certainly not stupid! I admit I am not perfect, but I am not stupid!*

5. **Old and harmful habits of thought can be replaced by new constructive ones.** Monica might develop the

habit of thinking, *I can probably understand just about anything I want to understand.* The more often she repeats this idea, the more convincing it feels to her. With time, it might feel even more true than her old belief about being stupid.

6. **New habits of thought enable new habits of speech and behavior, and new choices.** Once Monica breaks her bad habit of thinking she is stupid, she might accept a friend's invitation to join a book club. She might speak up during the meetings in a cheerful and confident way. Other members might praise her for her insights. A whole new world starts to open up for Monica.

7. **Once the desired new habits of thought are clear, changes in habitual speech and behavior can support the new habits of thought.** Monica is now deeply committed to feeling better about herself. She realizes that she still thinks of herself as stupid at times, particularly when she is stressed. She decides to take a college course and work hard for a good grade. She realizes this behavior is incompatible with her old belief that she is stupid, which helps her defeat this bad habit of thinking.

8. **Understanding the historical origins of a harmful belief can be worthwhile, but isn't absolutely necessary for success.** In psychotherapy, Monica might recall being called stupid by a mean-spirited, alcoholic stepfather during the early years of her life. If she can understand that these insults were completely arbitrary, she might become somewhat more able to dispute her present beliefs about her stupidity. However, Monica doesn't *need* to unearth the historical origins of her beliefs to overcome them.

9. **The most reliable and effective way to relieve problems such as depression, anger, and anxiety is to alter harmful habits of thought.** Monica no longer believes she is stupid. She doesn't think she is a genius either, but she feels about as intellectually capable as other people. Monica is content with this outcome. Because feeling stupid was the biggest source of sorrow in her life, she feels much better. In fact, she no longer suffers from sadness, fatigue, anxiety, and sleep disturbance the way she used to.

Methods like these, some employed by therapists, others employed in self-help, have enabled millions of people to overcome anxiety, depression, and other problems. Monica's voyage toward greater happiness and productivity might have been self-coached, or she might have been coached by a psychotherapist. In either case, the principles and methods would have been about the same.

I would be presumptuous to assert that cognitive psychotherapy is the best of all possible approaches to psychotherapy. Some intelligent and well-meaning psychotherapists completely reject it. Others use it primarily to supplement other approaches such as psychoanalytic methods. Still, cognitive psychotherapy is by far the best supported by science at this time. Scientific research has confirmed the value of cognitive methods, while science and history have not been so kind to other approaches to psychotherapy.

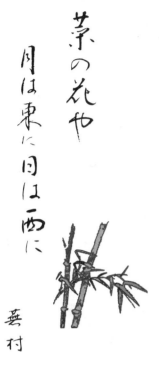

2

A Cognitive Approach to Wanting What You Have

Psychotherapy focuses on the habitual thoughts that evoke depression, anxiety, or anger.

In this workbook, I focus on habitual thoughts that support wanting what you have; I also identify habitual thoughts and beliefs that prevent or discourage wanting what you have.

The goal of wanting what you have is much broader than the goal of psychotherapy, which is primarily to treat symptoms and relieve suffering. The goals of wanting what you have are: greater enjoyment of life and the people around us; greater serenity about disappointments, losses, and misfortunes; more kindness and empathy for the people around us, and less blame and judgment; a more ethical and environmentally responsible way of life; and greater appreciation for life's depth.

These goals are related in some ways to depression and anxiety, in that great success might reduce or even cure some emotional disorders or prevent their recurrence. Nevertheless, treatment of emotional disorders is not the primary purpose for practicing Compassion, Attention, and Gratitude.

What Exactly Does "Wanting What You Have" Mean?

"Wanting what you have" is a slogan I've chosen for a particular reason. Many New Age ideas and slogans emphasize unorthodox ways of getting what you want that are based on the assumption that getting what you want will make you happy and make you a better person. Some New Age ideas suggest that spiritual growth is rewarded by increased love, prosperity, or status, or maybe all three. I wanted to set a different tone.

Although I have some misgivings about pie-in-the-sky philosophy, I do assume that my readers value success and strive for it. I take it for granted that my readers are responsible, loving parents and good citizens. If you have big problems with underachievement or laziness, you might be reading the wrong book.

On the other hand, I don't promise that my readers will increase their incomes, invigorate their sex lives, or amplify their charisma by wanting what they have. Neither do I assume that my readers would be better off if they could do these things. There are very good reasons to think that increased income or sexual magnetism wouldn't increase the quality of my readers' lives. I know that this is a surprising statement, and I'll explain it further in chapter 4.

I could have chosen some other slogan. "Want what you have" *might* have been any of the following:

Be here now.

Practice mindfulness.

Today is the first day of the rest of your life.

The kingdom of God is within you.

Imitate Christ.

This is the precious present.

Surrender your problems to a higher power.

Have a nice day.

I chose "Learn to want what you have" instead because:

- It's nonreligious, but not antireligious. In this way, it makes common ground for atheists, traditional believers, and nonreligious people who consider themselves spiritual.

- It accents pleasure and good cheer rather than self-denial.

- It encourages moderation in habits and desires while implicitly acknowledging the harm done by greed and self-importance.

- It reminds us that means count more than ends.

- It emphasizes the value of the present over the past and the future.

- It requires no dramatic change in lifestyle.

- It connects life's depth to ordinary existence. Life's magic and grandeur are not located in the future or in an alternate reality—they're right here, right now.

As I mentioned in the previous chapter, my approach to wanting what you have is to emphasize the systematic practice of Compassion, Attention, and Gratitude, three separate but related principles. When I write about wanting what you have, I always mean the practice of Compassion, Attention, and Gratitude, which, for convenience, I often abbreviate as C, A, and G.

Compassion, Attention, and Gratitude are excellent principles for wanting what you have because, with just a little explanation, they are easily understood and can be put into practice immediately—at any time and any place. In particular, they are best understood in terms of thinking habits, just as Monica's depression (in chapter 1) is easiest to understand in terms of Monica's thinking habits.

In the same way, I am going to explain Compassion, Attention, and Gratitude in terms of habitual thoughts and their behavioral and emotional consequences. Most importantly, I will repeatedly teach the fundamentals and occasionally help you with the fine points of your technique. The fundamentals are these:

- discovering how a lifetime of craving the things you don't have, and may never have, harms your quality of life as well as the quality of life for the people around you

- discovering false and harmful habits of thinking about the good things you now possess, which time and chance will inevitably take away from you

- learning that you, just like everyone else, persistently crave *more*: you crave *more* wealth, *more* status, and *more* love

- learning that the persistent and insistent craving for *more* can be managed just like any other harmful habit of thinking

- critically examining your persistent desires for more, and then disputing them

- developing new habits of thought to take the place of your usual desires

- practicing these new habits of thought in many settings and in relation to many of life's problems

- discovering new habits of speech and behavior to support your new habits of thought

- learning to notice and appreciate the practical, emotional, and spiritual benefits of your new habits of thought

Compassionate Habits of Thought

Compassionate habits of thought recognize the uniqueness and importance of each person—even unpleasant or dangerous people. They remind us that no one *deserves* pain or joy, success or failure. These things are often dictated by chance. Even when punishment or retaliation is socially necessary, we need not hate anyone. When thinking compassionately, we remember that most of the time we can enjoy most of the people around us—we can even learn from or be inspired by them.

Attentive Habits of Thought

Attentive habits of thought recognize the value and uniqueness of the present moment. Joy lives in the present, not the past or the future. Too much ambition or nostalgia takes the joy out of life. In practicing Attention, we learn not to damage or demean the present moment by making unnecessary value judgments about the way things are. We learn acceptance and serenity about a world that is necessarily imperfect. In fact, we learn that a perfect world is impossible and undesirable. In some cases, we can learn to enjoy life's problems and imperfections.

Grateful Habits of Thought

Grateful habits of thought recognize the many good things we already possess. We learn not to take them for granted and to derive joy from them, even if they seem ordinary and familiar. We learn that habitual grateful thoughts moderate the restless greed that comes from instinctive human desires for more.

What's Next

In chapter 3, I'll try to inspire you by pointing out the benefits of wanting what you have and the problems associated with a lifetime of craving what you don't have. Following that, in chapter 4, I'll examine the insistent, relentless desire for more, and its instinctive and universally human origins. In chapters 5 through 8, I'll begin to describe the fundamentals of wanting what you have: Compassion, Attention, and Gratitude. I'll describe each one primarily in terms of habitual thoughts and beliefs.

In chapters 9 through 17, I'll describe how the three principles can be used as problem-solving tools in a wide variety of problem situations. In chapter 18, I'll provide logs, checklists, problem-solving forms, and other devices that you can use to keep your practice of Compassion, Attention, and Gratitude fresh and inspiring for as long as you like.

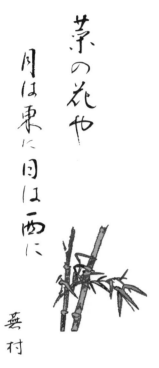

3

The Magic and Grandeur of Ordinary Existence

The intent of this chapter is to inspire you—to help you imagine how your life could be better, and how you could be better, if you learned to want what you have.

The Pleasure Planet

This exercise was inspired by Harlan Ellison's short story "Strange Wine." In the story, a man kills himself at the end of a life that most people would consider sorrowful and lonely. His job was tedious, his marriage was tedious, and one of his children had died. After death, he finds himself on a grim, nearly featureless planet inhabited by ugly crablike beings. He recalls that he lived on this planet once, as one of these crablike beings, before he was sent to spend a lifetime on Earth as a human being.

He asks what crime he committed to justify a sentence so harsh as his life on Earth. He is told that Earth is the "pleasure planet," a place where there is more joy and less suffering than anywhere else in the known universe. He was sent to live a lifetime on Earth as a reward for his exemplary behavior.

The story ends on an impressionistic but touching note: "... and he knew that they had given him the only gift of joy permitted to the races of beings who lived in the far galaxies. The gift of a few precious years on a world where anguish was so much less than known everywhere else. He remembered the rain, and the sleep, and the feel of beach sand beneath his feet, and ocean rolling in to whisper its eternal song, and on just such nights as those he had despised on Earth, he slept and dreamed good dreams of life on the pleasure planet."

This man was unable to recognize the pleasure planet until it was too late. Nevertheless, he could now remember his experiences as pleasurable even though he did not see the beauty and joy the first time around. He could not see them because he was preoccupied by what he wanted and often ignored or devalued what he had.

This story points the way to wanting what you have. As a matter of fact, I think this story was one of my first inspirations for wanting what I have; I heard it from a client in 1983. The story challenges us to imagine how its main character would have thought differently if he had known he was granted the privilege of one lifetime in human form on the pleasure planet. It also challenges us to rethink our own lives and question our own assumptions. Accept the challenge. Try the following exercise.

Imagine that you have just met some genuine extraterrestrial creatures, obviously wise, kind, and technically advanced, who happened to land in your backyard without being detected by the Air Force. They show you several amazing things and tell you many more. By far their most surprising piece of news is that many alien creatures do experience a kind of reincarnation. If they live particularly noble and admirable lives, they are allowed to be reborn on the pleasure planet and spend one lifetime there. This is a planet where pain is less hurtful than anywhere else in the known universe, where there is more love and kindness than anywhere else, where natural beauties are more glorious and abundant, and where the mysteries are more subtle. Naturally, you ask them where this planet is, and they say to you, "It's Earth, of course. Didn't you know that?"

Spend some time digesting this fantasy then ask yourself the following questions. Spend a few minutes patiently contemplating each one. Make a mental note of your answers.

1. Look around your present surroundings. How might you see them, taste them, and smell them differently if you were certain you live on the pleasure planet?

2. How would you think and feel differently about the important people in your life if you were certain that Earth is the pleasure planet?

3. Reflect upon the simple pleasures you have enjoyed over the years: laughter, sex, affection, play, jobs well done, good food eaten, companionship shared, and so on. Do they take on a different character if you pretend that these are supreme pleasures?

4. Imagine how your thoughts and emotions would work differently if you spent the rest of your life completely convinced that Earth is the pleasure planet. Would you be worse off or better off, emotionally and practically, than you are now?

For future reference, record the thoughts and feelings that arose in the course of this exercise:

_____

_____

_____

_____

_____

Angela, one of my previewers, made the following notes after doing this exercise.

It took me a minute to warm up to this, until I remembered what it was like to play "pretend" when I was a child. When I just "played pretend," it was fun. Right away I thought about how much I take long warm hugs for granted, and also sex and orgasms, and also good red wine and smelly cheese. Those are a few of my favorite things. (Sorry, Julie Andrews.) I didn't find it difficult to believe that these are ultra-extra-special unique pleasures. When I thought about really believing the pleasure planet thing for the rest of my life, I balked at first, but that was because I was imagining what would happen if I tried to tell everybody. But what if I knew it, and just kept quiet about it? I don't really see a problem. I'd still go to work, and I'd still go to the dentist, but I guess most days I'd feel lucky to have a chance to do those things. I'd also know when to stop working and stop worrying about my dental bills, because I'd value all the other great things there are to do.

A previewer named Robert had a very different reaction. He wrote, "I liked this exercise in some ways. In other ways, it depressed me. I looked around my life and thought, 'Is this as good as it gets?'"

Robert did not quite get the point. The main character in Ellison's story had the same doubts and ended up killing himself because he had not seen the beauty and mystery all around him. He did not see it because he did not *expect* to see it. His habits of thought concealed life's beauty and mystery from him. But once he *expected* to see the beauty and mystery of his life, he could see it quite clearly, though by then it was only a memory.

To Robert I would reply, "The circumstances of your life, both good and bad, may not ever be better than they are now. Your challenge is to find satisfaction and meaning in your life *as it is.* If your life as it is seems disappointing and unlikely to change, you need not be discouraged but you do need to see your life with new eyes."

These Are the Good Old Days

The next two exercises don't require as much imagination, but for most people they are just as powerful.

In the following space, list the good things you now have in your life that you once longed to possess but perhaps feared you never would.

The Good Things

_____

_____

_____

_____

_____

Now, suppose that a time will come in your life when you will remember days just like today with nostalgia. Suppose you might think, "Oh, those were the good old days. I didn't know how good they were. I wish I had them to live over again, so I could appreciate them properly." In the following space, write down the good things you now have in your life that you might someday feel nostalgic for.

Nostalgia for Now

_____

_____

_____

_____

_____

Angela made the following notes:

The good things I once hoped for that I now have include: A good music collection. Many friends. Two beautiful, happy, loving, smart children. An affectionate husband who doesn't lie to me and doesn't complain about doing the dishes. A friendly relationship with my Mom. An interesting job that isn't socially or environmentally harmful. I could go on all day, but these are some of the first ones that come to me.

The things in my present life I will some day be nostalgic for are: I am pretty athletic. I go to some good parties. I feel young. I look young—well, youngish. My children are good-natured and affectionate most of the time. When they bring home some little crafts project from school, their eyes just burn with love and pride. I cry when I think of it.

The Face of God

In one way or another, every major religion teaches us about the divinity of every person or, in some cases, of every living thing. Some religions teach that humans were made in God's image. Some emphasize the eternal soul. Others believe that consciousness is a piece of God's mind, temporarily residing in a person. Abstract arguments about which doctrine is correct don't seem very productive. They are all infinitely debatable, and all such arguments completely miss the main point.

The main point is that we, as ordinary human beings, have the ability to sense, somehow, the divinity of every other person. To be poetical about it, we have the ability, in theory, to look into the face of any living thing and see the face of God.

In practice, however, few people routinely see the face of God in the people around them, in the same way that Ellison's character failed to perceive that he was living on the pleasure planet until it was too late.

Most people *occasionally* apprehend the divinity of ordinary people. Such insights are often inspired by religious worship, movies, poems, songs, plays, drugs, or by special moments of deep intimacy with a loved one. For most people, these moments occur quite rarely. Why? Because few people ever try to experience the divinity in others. Those few who think about it usually don't have any definite method for achieving this kind of awareness. Drugs (LSD, for example) have been used for this purpose, but the results are unpredictable and it seems that the insights gained through LSD-induced revelations are soon forgotten.

The purpose of this chapter is to inspire readers to want what they have, and this includes the people who surround you. If you desire, and if your efforts are persistent, you can learn to appreciate the people you have in your present life.

For this exercise, choose a particular person to focus your attention on. Don't choose someone you love or hate. Instead, choose someone you know fairly well, about whom you don't have strong feelings. Imagine this person as vividly as possible in each of the following situations. Of course you will imagine the face, but there is much more to a person than a face: also imagine the person's body movements, the sound and rhythm of his speech, his choice of words, if any, even his heart rate and respiration.

Imagine this person:

- Naked, in the arms of his mother, a few minutes after birth

- As a child about six years old, during a playful, carefree moment

- Performing an act of selfless kindness

- Gazing into the eyes of someone he loves, or used to love

- During a moment of despair

- During a moment of deep personal pride

- During a moment of profound pain

- Breathing his last few breaths as he dies

Record in the following lines how your feelings about this person changed as a result of doing this exercise. If your view of people in general seemed to change, record this as well.

_____

_____

_____

_____

_____

Cyara wrote the following.

I thought of a woman I have worked with in the same office for twelve years. I speak to her almost every day. Over the years I have gotten to know her pretty well. I can't say I like or don't like her. She probably feels the same way about me. The first few visualizations just blew away all the little categories I had put her into. It just stopped mattering whether I thought she is dumb or smart, charming or crass. I realized that I had pigeon-holed her, based on how well she fitted into my plans. It has never before occurred to me that I might not fit very well into her plans. I felt somewhat ashamed of the shallow, selfish ways I treat her. I imagined I was seeing her the way God would see her, if I believed in God, which I don't. But I liked seeing her that way anyway. The next time I met her, I felt I was in a state of grace. I'll slip back to my old habits, but I hope to keep rediscovering these things in her and everyone else until I can always remember.

This chapter was intended to give you a seat-of-the-pants impression of how your life might feel different if you began to seriously study the art of wanting what you have. Briefly review the exercises you've done in the chapter as well as the experiences they evoked. If you've been inspired, make a note of your inspiration so that you can reawaken it later, if needed.

Notes

_____

_____

_____

_____

_____

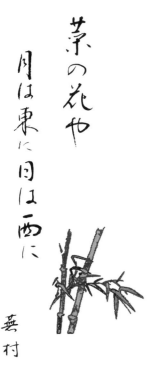

4

Endless Craving

Buddha's "First Noble Truth" is that all living things suffer. His second noble truth is that the cause of suffering is desire. This teaching is repeated many times in more familiar Judeo-Christian traditions. Christ's teachings in this respect were not too different, though he was a bit more specific. He emphasized more particular desires, such as the desire for revenge, the desire for wealth, lust for thy neighbor's spouse, and so on.

The problem is not desire itself, because desire and its gratification can certainly be joyful. Babies are conceived in happy mutual lust. You desire a trip to the mountains, you make plans, you go, you have a great time. What's the problem?

The problem is that desire has no end. No matter how many of your desires you satisfy, new ones pop up to take the place of the old. If you satisfy all your inexpensive desires, you'll develop expensive ones. If you are educated, you'll want to be better educated. If you satisfy your modest ambitions, you'll develop grand ambitions. If your children are bright, you'll want them to be brilliant. If they're brilliant, you'll want them to win the Nobel prize. If you get plastic surgery to make yourself look better, you'll decide you don't look good enough yet.

This, then, is the challenge: to know that you are not your desires; you can decide what kind of relationship you will have with your desires. Nature gives every person a huge number of desires. Everybody gets the same basic set, with a little bit of variation from one person to another. Desires are merely impersonal natural forces working within your physical body and brain chemistry.

For example, most healthy adults crave sexual activity from time to time. Yet people with similar sexual desires make different choices about how to manage them. Some choices are wise, some are not; some bring joy, some bring misery. Some sexual choices bring so much misery into the world that it makes a lot of sense to call them sins.

This is the beginning of a cognitive model for wanting what you have. An essential first step is to identify habits of thinking that are incompatible with wanting what you have. This task is emotionally difficult because you must reconsider some of your deepest and most treasured beliefs.

Consider how many of your deeply held thoughts and beliefs take some of these forms:

If I can never have _____ , it will be very hard to be happy and contented. Instead, I will probably feel _____ .

If I can never achieve _____ , it will be very hard to be happy and contented. Instead, I will probably feel _____ .

If I can never experience _____ , it will be very hard to be happy and contented. Instead, I will probably feel _____ .

If I have to keep on doing _____ , it will be very hard to be happy and contented. Instead, I'll probably feel _____ .

If, one day, I am no longer able to _____ , it will be very hard to be happy and contented. Instead, I'll probably feel _____ .

If I one day, I lose _____ , it will be very hard to be happy and contented. Instead, I'll probably feel _____ .

In subsequent chapters, you'll inventory many ways you could fill in these blanks. For now, just think of a few ways you would fill in these blanks—maybe just one instance per item. Think about it, then record your reactions here:

_____

_____

_____

_____

Sylvia wrote the following.

When I look at my desires this way, it is pretty easy to see that Buddha wasn't just whistling Dixie when he said that desires are the cause of suffering. Let's see . . . if I can never have the kind of slender body I dream of, I'll be unhappy. If I can never achieve financial independence, I'll be unhappy. If I can never experience genuine affection and sympathy from my father, I'll be unhappy. If I have to keep on working at my job, which started out as a "get-by job" six years ago, I'll be unhappy. It just goes on and on. It's as though I have this psychic ability to predict the future, and I am predicting my own unhappiness—misery even!

Buddha's first noble truth can be translated another way: "life is uncertain." This makes more sense. It's not *entirely* true that all living things suffer. Most people, all over the world, report they are "pretty happy" or "very happy," unless they are seriously ill or starving.

Buddha may have intended to contrast the relentlessness of our desires with the uncertainty of life. He may have meant to say, "Life is uncertain. Yet, in our thoughts, we demand certainty. That leaves all humans in a very awkward position."

Sylvia wants to feel certain that she will one day have the thin, athletic body she has dreamed of having for many years. She wants to feel sure that one day, while she is still young enough to enjoy it, she will achieve financial independence. To be disappointed in these ways seems *unacceptable* to Sylvia. Part of the problem is that, in our minds, desires become *needs* and needs become *rights*. Sylvia begins early adulthood with the desire for financial independence. Her failure to achieve it troubles her, and she doesn't like that feeling. Soon, in her habits of thought, she *needs* to become financially independent. The thought of remaining indefinitely frustrated about her limited finances becomes unbearable. She sees that other people, less worthy and less deserving than she, have somehow achieved financial independence. Why can't she? If they can have it, she has a right to have it too. So, when Sylvia's desire remains frustrated, she feels that something precious has been stolen from her. She feels a grudge. She may feel simmering outrage, or despair, or both.

The human situation—relentless desires colliding with profound uncertainty—produces vast consequences. Following is just a small representative sample of those consequences:

- Limited ability to enjoy the other people

- Limited ability to be kind or generous

- Greed, or willingness to harm innocent others, for the sake of success

- Dread of loss, dread of loneliness

- Boredom or restlessness

- Excessive dependence upon the approval of others

- Fear of death, avoidance of thoughts of death

- Fears, regrets, and resentments, accumulating with advancing age

- Doubt about whether life is really worth all the trouble

- Lukewarm enjoyment of life

- A sense of not having lived fully, or a sense that one's cup has not yet been filled

- A sense that one has overlooked most of the fun, beauty, and mystery, and is likely to continue doing so

- A sense that life's depth has opened its doors to others, but not to you

- Willingness to submit to misguided politicians or dictators who promise all your dreams will soon come true

- Willingness to submit to misguided or self-destructive religious beliefs that promise all your dreams will soon come true

People with troubles like these don't suffer all the time. On many days, they might say that they are pretty happy. Still, it seems that they have failed to master the human situation. I'll explore these concerns in subsequent chapters. For now, the goal is to get a clearer idea of what the problem is.

The Geography of Craving

People crave so many different things in so many different ways that it seems impossible to understand the big picture. But if we can better understand people in general, we can better understand ourselves.

People naturally want to survive more than anything else. Needs for water, food, shelter, and protection from immediate dangers always come first. Beyond that people want the prerequisites for reproductive success, which can be easily summarized as the desire for wealth, status, and love.

Wealth

Wealth is not just money; wealth is the things that money can buy. The most important things it buys are healthy and varied food, good medical care, rest and physical comfort, amusement, education, conveniences, good child care, personal assistance, favors, access to new opportunities to get even richer, and so on. In a nonmoney society, some people will have more access to these things than others, and they can reasonably be considered richer.

If you have little or no desire for wealth, you are either an unusual person or you don't know yourself very well. Don't think of wealth simply as money in the bank or an expensive car. Look over the previous paragraph and identify some of the good things you crave that are hard to come by without money. Make a record below for future reference.

Forms of Wealth I Desire

Item	Intensity (1 = very mild; 10 = very strong)

Status

Status seems complicated, particularly in the United States, because there are so many subcultures. A hero in one subculture might be a geek in another. Nonetheless, it's easy to see who has more or less status in any given society. When you have status, you are treated with deference. If people dislike you, they hide their feelings. Many others admire you simply because you have power. Some will fear you simply because you have power. You have the power to make the rules—to decide who gets the rewards and who gets the punishment.

Status can take quirky forms. I have seen subcultures in which people compete to be the most modest or the most self-destructive. Such oddities are inexplicable except in the context of the subculture. The fraternity brat who drinks most self-destructively and fights most often with the police may win genuine status among his peers. If this behavior no longer gave him status among his peers, he'd stop doing it.

Most people will insist that they have no interest in status. Yet who doesn't wish to be admired? Who has never wished he could improve the world according to his specifications? Who has never wished for more deference from others? As I become immersed in the subculture of married, middle-aged, middle-class white guys, it's increasingly (and painfully) apparent that much of what passes for friendship is actually a mutual deference arrangement. Genuine affection and loyalty seem rare.

Look again at the previous paragraph about status. Take a deep breath and give it some thought. Identify some of the ways you hope for more status. Make a record below for future reference.

Forms of Status I Desire

Item	Intensity (1 = very mild; 10 = very strong)

Love

Love naturally includes romantic and sexual love, but it doesn't stop there. A good friend will go to great lengths for a friend she loves. The loyalty and generosity of parents, siblings, and other relatives are valuable and emotionally satisfying forms of love. A hero may be loved for the sacrifices he has made for the benefit of all.

A happily married woman, with happy, healthy, children and good relations with her parents, might imagine she has no further need for love. If it's true, she's an unusual person. More likely, she needs to know herself better. Is she entirely satisfied with the way her friends, neighbors, and relatives treat her? Does she want to be more widely acknowledged as a good person? Does she want her children to be more grateful for all the good things she does for them? Does she want her husband to be more romantic and perhaps a bit more eager in the bedroom? Chances are, the answers are yes, yes, yes, and yes.

Look over this discussion of love and identify the forms of love you most crave. Make a record below for future reference.

Forms of Love I Desire

Item	Intensity (1 = very mild; 10 = very strong)

The Lottery Exercise

Some scientists devote their careers to the study of happiness and unhappiness. They have found that the average person who wins a large sum of money in a lottery or sweepstakes generally ends up somewhat less happy than he was before he won. A surprisingly large percentage end up wishing they'd never won.

You know the reply to this factoid, don't you? Repeat after me ... *These people don't know where to shop!*

But seriously, try mentioning this fact at any social gathering. Most people refuse to believe it. Many will say, "That might be true of others, but I assure you, *I* would enjoy *my* winnings tremendously."

What's going on here? People protect their fondest desires from the difficult facts of life. A good way to do that is simply to ignore the difficult facts of life. That's what your audience is doing when you tell them of lotteries and happiness. In your heart, do you not yourself believe that you would be the exception to the rule? Don't you believe that you would enjoy your winnings tremendously, too? If so, that doesn't make you a jerk. It just makes you human. In preparation to dispute and revise your deepest beliefs about your reasons for living, consider the lottery question more carefully and from a very personal perspective.

This lottery exercise may seem unduly pessimistic. Yet optimism and pessimism both take many forms. If this were the end of it, the exercise would indeed be a cynical one. But this isn't the end. It's the beginning. In the meantime, the good news is that you'll never again have to feel disappointed about not winning the lottery.

Self-Examination

If you're like most people, it's disturbing to recognize how many desires you have and how intense they are. It's even more disturbing to recognize how many will remain unrequited. Yet the purpose of these experiments is not just to make you squirm. In chapter 1, Monica had to confront her sincere belief that she is stupid before she could question it and then dispute it. Once she disputed her misguided belief, she was able to substitute a more realistic and cheerful belief and make that belief a new habit. Once she succeeded, she felt much better. In a similar way, your goal is to discover the habits of thought that needlessly multiply your desires and intensify your distress when they are frustrated.

In the following exercise, you will find an assortment of things that might happen if you were to win several million dollars in the lottery. Don't work at this too hard. With a light heart and an open mind, read through them and rate the likelihood of each event. For your convenience, and also for the sake of making a point, the various possibilities are arranged in two columns, one for good items, the other for bad items.

1 = very likely
3 = neutral or undecided
5 = very unlikely

Good Outcomes	Likelihood	Bad Outcomes	Likelihood
My friends and relatives start discovering all my good qualities.		I start comparing my nice new clothes to those worn by really fashionable people. I feel more shabby than before.	
My kids become more cooperative and more interested in their school work.		I buy a great stereo and lots of CDs I always wanted to own, but don't often listen to them.	
My marriage becomes more tender, romantic, and sexy.		I buy a large-screen TV, but realize the same old junk looks worse when it's bigger.	
A new swimming pool, kitchen, car, and wardrobe give me lasting happiness.		I find myself less able to be close to the people around me than I was before, because I don't know whether they actually like me or are just interested in my money.	
I am able to buy plenty of expensive medicine, plastic surgery, and vitamins, and go to the gym quite often. As a result, I feel young again.		I run out of money before I buy half the stuff I want to buy or help half the people I want to help, and end up more worried about money than I was before.	

I stop worrying about my health. I stop worrying about aging and death. I stop worrying about my fading youth and attractiveness.		I travel to exotic locations just to find myself ensnared in one tourist trap after another.	
I no longer get sad the way I used to. I no longer feel misunderstood or taken for granted.		I discover lots of new, compelling desires for things that not even a lottery winner can afford.	

Powerful, persistent desires for things that will never be is not just your problem, it is a universal human problem. In subsequent chapters you'll learn how to take a new perspective on your desires in a way that I hope will improve the quality of your life and make you a kinder and more compassionate person.

Hindu and Buddhist traditions encourage us to renounce desire. Judeo-Christian tradition emphasizes sinful desires, but the basic idea is about the same. Many people find this suggestion impossible, because they believe that desires are not under voluntary control, that there is no On or Off switch.

Some find the idea of renunciation joyless or forbidding. They ask themselves, quite rightly, "If I renounce the desire for a chocolate milkshake, will I still enjoy chocolate milkshakes? Will I ever bother to drink one again? If I renounce all of my desires, where will my pleasures and joys come from?"

The following exercise is a more user-friendly way of understanding renunciation.

Review the incomplete sentences you filled in on page 24. Recall your reactions, and review your notes. Focus your attention on one of the items you gave thought to and write it again here:

_____

_____

_____

_____

Now imagine that you could take a magic pill that would instantly and effortlessly alter this habit of thought. After taking the pill, you will remain able to pursue your goal and enjoy its attainment, if attainment is possible. What will change is your expectation that you will be very unhappy if you do not attain it.

How are you different after you take the pill? Take your time with this. Let the fantasy grow in vividness and detail. Don't try to direct your thoughts. Instead, let the fantasy take on a life of its own. Record your reaction here:

_____

_____

_____

_____

Sylvia had written,

If I never achieve financial independence, I'll find it very hard to be happy and contented. In fact, I'll probably feel humiliated and anxious, even panicky. I might get depressed too, because I won't be able to do all the fun things I've always looked forward to doing someday.

After doing this exercise, Sylvia wrote,

Okay, after I take the pill (it's tiny, oval, and very hard—it glows pale green in the dark), my thoughts go like this. Life is uncertain. Maybe I'll achieve financial independence and maybe I won't. There will be plenty of good things to enjoy either way. If some people think less of me because of my thrift-shop furniture, that's their problem. If my brothers and sisters look down on me because I have to ask Mom for a check every once in awhile, I don't have to take them seriously. If I don't take these things so seriously, I might have more time for more deeply satisfying friendships. In any case, I know it is within my power to be happy and to enjoy life working at a Burger King, if that's what I have to do to survive. Thinking this way makes me feel calmer. I notice the clouds outside my window. I notice how much I like the music playing on my radio.

If renunciation meant giving up your tastes, interests, talents, and pleasures, no one would do it. Of course, that isn't possible anyway, as far as I can tell. The few people I've met who seem to have renounced all interests and pleasures were chronic schizophrenic, and they were not enlightened. Their lives were a continuing torment.

Think of renunciation as giving up the habit of thought that says, *I must have it. Without it, I can't possibly be happy.*

5

Compassion

菜の花や
月は東に日は西に

蕪村

In common usage, "Compassion" means many different things: feeling vicarious sorrow for another person's misfortune; empathizing—experiencing someone else's difficulties from her point of view; trying to offer assistance to people one might not even know, such as cancer patients or the homeless; trying to influence someone else for his own good, such as discouraging alcohol abuse or bringing Christianity to the infidel; or forgiving the unforgivable, as when a victim's family pleads for clemency for the murderer.

I don't necessarily intend any of these meanings when I use the word Compassion in this book.

When I talk about Compassion, I refer to a set of related habits of thought and habits of action and speech that revolve around the theme of Compassion. Thus, my version of Compassion is complex and not amenable to a brief definition. I will begin to explain my definition here from a cognitive perspective, and at the end of this chapter I'll attempt a more straightforward definition, though it won't be short.

On pages 6–7, Monica discovered that her habit of thinking of herself as stupid was incompatible with her happiness and productivity. In the same way, you can identify common habits of thought incompatible with the practice of Compassion. Because Compassion is a broad topic I cannot identify all the forms of uncompassionate thoughts, but I can identify some broad themes and representative examples.

She doesn't deserve all the good things that happen to her.	
He deserves to suffer.	
Anybody that stupid deserves whatever happens to him.	
That person's life is a waste. He's not worth the air he breathes.	
He's a failure and always will be.	
What can you do with an idiot/psycho/jerk/creep like that?	
I don't care whether she lives or dies.	
She only has herself to blame.	
He has no right to be so stupid (or selfish, stubborn, unreasonable, and so on).	
She has no right to inconvenience me like this.	
I hate the way he's so arrogant, like he knows everything.	
I hate her condescension. Some day she'll find out what I really think of her.	
He should try to be more reasonable. No wonder he has so many enemies.	
He enjoys fouling his own nest!	
He likes to make people hate him.	
He only feels comfortable when others are uncomfortable.	

You're probably wondering what the blank right-hand column is for. Surprise! Go back and after each item write a rough estimate (such as "never" or "once or twice") of how many times in a typical month you have a similar thought. Make note of the ones you actually say to other people.

Most uncompassionate thoughts fall into one or more of the following categories:

- Wishing harm or misery upon another person

- Blanket condemnations of another person

- Wishing to "help along" the natural consequences arising from another person's poor judgment

- Deliberately nursing hatred or contempt for another person

- Declaring another person "unworthy" of some desirable circumstance

- Planning revenge

- Encouraging others to think, speak, or act in uncompassionate ways

- Hoping or planning to humiliate or harm someone

- Deliberately exaggerating a person's bad qualities while failing to consider the good ones

- Attributing differences of opinion to the other person's stupidity, ignorance, or mental illness

- Attributing another person's errors in judgment to stupidity or mental illness

- Unwillingness to admit that the other person might be right and that you might be mistaken

- Taking pleasure in the sorrow and misfortune of others

In the same way that Monica first questioned her habitual idea that she is stupid, you might question the habitual idea that thinking and speaking in this manner is necessary, useful, or decent. Uncompassionate thinking is harmful not just to others but to yourself—when you think uncompassionately you make the world seem more ugly, more pointless, more lonely, and more chaotic than it would seem to you otherwise. This kind of thinking will often be expressed in your speech and in this way you make yourself less likable; you discourage the sympathy others might feel for you in the future. If you speak disparagingly about others, even in private to your friends, your friends will wonder when they will be on the receiving end of the same kind of condemnation. Uncompassionate thinking will make you resentful about the occasional necessity to help or forgive someone to whom you owe a favor, and even more resentful about sometimes having to assist or forgive a stranger, to whom you owe no favors. Eventually, uncompassionate thinking will cause you to envy and resent people whose lives seem more fortunate than yours.

In similar ways, uncompassionate thinking alters the social atmosphere around you in mildly toxic ways. By setting bad examples, you unwittingly encourage others to think uncompassionately. You never know; you may one day have a dispute with someone in whom you have previously sewn an uncompassionate seed. You may regret it.

Uncompassionate thinking, and related uncompassionate speech and behavior, harms the people you love the most because your habitual patterns of thought will cause you to sometimes paint even the people you love with the same brush. They might view you as hardhearted, clueless, and brutish without your even being aware of it.

Finally, by thinking uncompassionately you harm the whole world for present and future generations. Uncompassionate thinking is contagious. So is compassionate thinking. Human history has had its share of uncompassionate thinking thus far, and the grisly results can be found in any history book. Is this the kind of world you want to bequeath to your great-great-grandchildren?

Is Compassion Practical?

People otherwise receptive to the concept of Compassion often ask what kind of world it would be if every murderer, rapist, thief, and reckless driver was forgiven instead of held responsible for his actions. Such a question indicates an imperfect understanding of Compassion.

Compassion does not require us to trust people who are not worthy of our trust; give spare change to winos, who perhaps will spend it self-destructively; ignore evil; allow evil people to harm innocent people; withhold assertiveness; or protect foolish people from the consequences of their actions. The Compassion I'm referring to is different from the kind of compassion that a parent feels for a child. Parents sometimes refuse to recognize the harm that their children have done. Parents sometimes try to protect their children from the natural consequences of their mistakes. Parental protectiveness like this is natural and understandable, but it is no model for the disciplined and principled practice of Compassion I refer to.

Compassion as I want to teach it is a pattern of thinking habits. It generates internal, private experiences that can be called compassionate. Compassion most consistently benefits the individual who practices it. Hatred, resentment, condemnation, anger, and other such emotions, which tend to interfere with good judgment and smart problem solving, become less frequent and less intense when you practice Compassion. In this sense, Compassion is very practical.

Additionally, if you often hate, condemn, resent, and so on, you inevitably diminish the quality of life not only for yourself but for the people around you—the people you love. You're unpleasant to be around if you're constantly wrathful about idiot motorists, the criminals at the IRS, the moronic coach of your favorite team, or the other objects of your frequent calumny. If practicing Compassion enhances quality of life for the people you love, it is practical indeed.

Somehow, skeptics about Compassion imagine that if Compassion were widely practiced, criminals would not be punished, bad manners would not be disapproved of, and lazy workers would not be disciplined. Yet if you carefully review the discussion of Compassion in this chapter and the introductory chapter, you'll find nothing that would discourage punishment of criminals. What you will find is that you are discouraged from hating criminals, thinking yourself superior to ill-mannered people, or wishing misery upon lazy workers. Police and judges who hate criminals do not perform their jobs any more effectively; they might even be less effective because they allow their angry emotions to rule them. Managers need not hate lazy workers in order to supervise them effectively. To the contrary, a poorly motivated worker who is treated with contempt by a manager is likely to work even more slowly in the future. Voters need not be wrathful to vote out a dishonest politician. In fact, wrathful voters sometimes approve unwise laws.

Firm rules and laws, fair punishments, incentives for good behavior, and good manners—these things are socially necessary. Widespread hatred or contempt are not socially necessary. More often than not, they do social harm.

Compassionate Habits of Thought

I've identified some habits of thought contrary to Compassion. The next two logical steps are to dispute them and formulate alternate compassionate thoughts, which can then be made habitual. Throughout the rest of this workbook, I'll develop some general principles for formulating new compassionate thoughts in various situations. Here's a fairly easy representative example.

Imagine a poverty-stricken fourteen-year-old boy from the housing project around the corner. He has threatened to beat up your thirteen-year-old son, and he has spray-painted gang graffiti on your fence. In the first column, I'll describe likely uncompassionate thoughts about him. In the next column, I'll dispute each uncompassionate thought in turn. In the last column, I'll suggest a more compassionate thought that might be used to replace the old one.

Uncompassionate Thought	Dispute	Alternate Compassionate Thought
I'd like to kick his delinquent butt until he begged for mercy.	That probably wouldn't do any good. I might get arrested. I wouldn't do it anyway. The hate only hurts me.	I must think of some way to prevent these problems in the future.
He has no right to behave this way. Who does he think he is?	Why do I waste my time thinking this way? He is who he is. Rights have little to do with it.	My anger will stimulate me to take steps to solve the problem.
He belongs behind bars!	I'm not sure that would make the neighborhood safer in the long run. It might not be a fair punishment, either.	I'll figure out a way to confront him with the harm he's done. If there is no way to do that, I'll consider other options.
He's just another worthless punk.	He's a child who lives in poverty. He may not be supervised properly. There may be a lot of trouble in his family.	He's a human being who's made me very angry. That's all I really know about him. If I like, I can learn more about him.

Notice that the new compassionate thoughts are not naive or disempowering. They do not contradict normal, spontaneous feelings of anger. To the contrary, they recognize angry feelings but redirect them in more constructive directions.

Christ's admonition to turn the other cheek, as described in the Book of Matthew, might be understood in a similar way. Although the story does not say that Christ was struck, this may well have occurred at some point in Christ's life.

From his teachings, we might infer how he would have filled out the Compassion chart.

Uncompassionate Thought	Dispute	Alternate Compassionate Thought
This man has insulted me and demeaned my teaching. This must not be allowed.	To those who understand my work, this man has demeaned and insulted only himself.	This man might learn an important lesson if I do not strike in return.
My followers will not respect me if I do not demand respect from others.	My mission is to teach Compassion to others. I must teach by example and hope for the best.	Some of my followers might respect a strong, manly counterattack, but they'll admire calm self-possession even more.
If I do not return the blow, he may hit me again and perhaps harm me.	He does not appear intent on injuring me or killing me. He seems to want only to humiliate me.	If he tries to harm me seriously, I'll consider my options.
This man must be punished for this illegal and disgraceful assault.	Punishment takes many forms. If this man remains prideful and arrogant, he will suffer greatly.	I'll let natural consequences do the punishing. Further, I think he wants to be a better man. Maybe I can teach him.

Once again, notice that Christ's hypothetical internal dialog is not naive. Neither is it self-destructive. One can imagine other circumstances where he would have thought and behaved quite differently. Unfortunately, in modern times, this gospel story has been distorted to mean we should tolerate any attack with a loving smile, regardless of the circumstances. This misconception is harmful in two ways: it leaves Compassion open to ridicule and it makes Compassion seem like an impossible model, far beyond the reach of the average person.

Try this exercise yourself. Choose a particular person and a particular incident to focus on. This exercise is easier with people you don't like, harder with people who don't like you. Start with ordinary people and incidents that have caused you deep anger or fear. (I recommend practicing on some easier examples before attempting Adolf Hitler or Napoleon Bonaparte.)

The person: _____

The situation: _____

Uncompassionate Thought	Dispute	Alternate Compassionate Thought

Compassion Defined

So far I have given examples of what Compassion is and isn't. Now I'll provide the more specific definition of Compassion that I promised earlier. It still won't be short.

Compassion is a habit of thinking that is deliberately cultivated and systematically practiced—preferably for a lifetime. It is not a destination but a way of traveling. Compassion often requires mental effort. Exercising this mental effort strengthens us mentally and spiritually. Compassion sometimes alleviates anger, but not always. Compassion sometimes evokes sympathy for others, but not always. Compassion usually produces a gentle, patient, and nonviolent approach to various problems and disputes, but not always. There is nothing in the principle of Compassion to prevent a person from harming someone to protect herself, or to protect an innocent other, if that is the best option. There is nothing in the principle of Compassion to prevent fair laws from being carried out in a fair way. Actually, Compassion requires that fair laws be fairly carried out. (Otherwise, all suffer.) Compassion elevates the importance of kindness, patience, setting a good example, and acknowledging possible good qualities in others who cause us difficulty. Compassion is most often practiced in relation to a particular person or creature, rather than toward people in general.

Compassion usually discourages revenge and retaliation, though not in all cases. Whenever possible, Compassion allows natural consequences to do their work when people misbehave. Compassion recognizes that anger is a natural and spontaneous emotion that does good as well as harm. The emotion of anger should be acknowledged and respected as it occurs. Anger should not be violently suppressed. In many cases, it is impossible to suppress one's feelings of anger, but the practice of Compassion often quells anger in a natural and healthy way. In any case, anger need not always be expressed in word or deed; sometimes it must be contained, patiently, pending developments. Compassion de-emphasizes abstract rights and emphasizes the importance of compassionate person-to-person encounters. When two people have a dispute, both sides have rights, and usually both sides feel their rights have been violated. Rights-based thinking may do more harm than good. Compassion recognizes the importance of fundamental human rights but does not specify what they are. Compassion is not self-abasement. Self-assertion can always be done compassionately and in fact is usually more effective that way. Ultimately, the principle of Compassion arises from deep understanding of the following:

- No person's desires are any more important than anyone else's, nor any less important.

- Few people knowingly do wrong.

- Everyone makes errors of judgment. Everyone occasionally speaks or acts out of anger.

- No one asks to be stupid. No one asks to be mentally ill or alcoholic. No one asks for her personality or circumstances of birth.

- Everybody wants approximately the same things (wealth, status, and love) for approximately the same reasons. No one ever feels they've received as much as they need and want. Everybody dreads losing the good things they have.

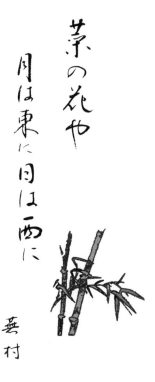

6

Attention

I intend "Attention" to mean about the same thing as what Buddhists call "mindfulness." I also intend it to mean approximately what Christians and Jews call "reverence" or "humility." I did not use these terms because they have cultural and religious connotations I wanted to avoid.

I began the previous chapter by explaining that Compassion, in common practice, means many different things. By contrast, terms such as "attention," "mindfulness," "reverence," and "humility" are heard so seldom that no one thinks much about what they mean. We might order a child to pay attention, or we might chide ourselves about inattention while working, studying, or driving, but these usages have little, if anything, to do with Attention the way I mean it.

As with Compassion, it's best to understand Attention as a habit of thinking. The following are some examples of habitual thoughts that contradict Attention.

I don't like this kind of weather. I wish it were hotter (cooler, drier, rainier, etc.).	
How could any sane person paint his house such a hideous shade of orange?	
If only I were taller (thinner, younger, older, etc.).	
Daffodils are nice, but I prefer roses.	
I wish we had some successful, charming friends, instead of all your loser buddies from high school and their trailer-trash wives.	
What a lovely sunset. It would be perfect without the mosquitoes.	
Why would anyone spoil such a nice, modern airport with that creepy New Age music?	
Can you believe it, she's actually a Jehovah's Witness (atheist, Unitarian, Baptist, etc.).	
Michael Jackson is okay, but I prefer the artist formerly known as Prince.	
She'd be so pretty if she got a nose job.	
Why won't he stop talking?	

For the most part, these examples demonstrate the following:

- complaining about or resenting things that are not likely to change

- deliberately making yourself uncomfortable by exaggerating the undesirable features of your surroundings

- cultivating a pleasant feeling of superiority relative to the people and things around you

- cultivating a stubborn insistence that the world adapt itself to your tastes and desires (a sense of entitlement)

- acting as a self-appointed judge of your surroundings, as if you were judging an art contest or a beauty pageant

- making needless comparisons—if a daffodil is before you and there are no roses around, there is no need to consider the rose a superior flower

Keeping this clarification in mind, return to the previous table and in the empty right-hand column indicate how often you make arbitrary value judgments similar to the ones described.

Questioning Nonattentive Thinking Habits

Nonattentive habits of thought involve an adversarial relationship with the here and now. Nonattentive thoughts say, in essence, *I'd rather be someplace else, doing something else.* Someplace else might include the past or future. We all do this occasionally, but to do it repetitively and willfully suggests disdain for the present. Here is where the connection to terms such as "reverence" and "humility" comes in. One can't be reverent or humble at the same time one is disdainful.

The consequences of nonattentive habits of thought are obvious: the world seems shabby and disappointing. Too often, the entire world seems to be an obstacle to where you'd like to be and what you'd like to be doing there. Other people seem to exist primarily for the purpose of offending or thwarting you. In this state of mind, loving yourself or anyone else seems very difficult. Being simply glad to be alive seems like a joke. By comparison, the past and future seem lovely and perfect, but frustratingly beyond reach. Additionally, nonattentive thoughts are deeply pessimistic: *There's nothing good going on around here, and it's not likely to get better soon. It's a shabby, shabby world, and the only escape from it is death.*

Joylessness and anxiety are the most serious consequences of nonattentive thinking. To illustrate: Let's say you can remember the cute way your little boy played when he was a baby, and you can also joyfully anticipate how proud you will be when he receives his Nobel prize. These daydreams might produce a brief, flickering glow of happiness. But they are nothing compared to the fact that right here, right now, you are home with your son, now a teenager. You can hug him, smell him, and hear his actual voice, which is much more clear and penetrating than the voice of memory. You don't know what he will say until he says it. If you smile, he might smile back.

Brooding

Brooding, living in the past in a mood of resentment or regret, is a habit of thought that contradicts Attention. Brooding is a major obstacle to joy in the lives of many people. A previewer named Frank examined his brooding habits and then questioned them:

Past Events I Brood About	Why It's Unnecessary
The time in ninth grade I got bullied and beat up in front of Georgine, and how she started going out with the bully and dumped me.	I have already learned my lesson from that experience. Further reflection produces no benefit. It happened. It's over.
My father could have been a lot more sensitive and patient.	I already understand that as well as it can be understood.
My car stereo got ripped off last month.	I am now taking all the extra precautions I'm going to take. I don't think it'll happen again. If it does, I'll deal with it.
My wife once met a male friend for lunch and tried to hide it from me.	I have this silly idea that if I go over it in my mind often enough I can figure out a way to understand exactly what happened and why. Even if I had a time machine, that would be impossible, and brooding makes a very poor time machine anyway.
I once made a really pointless and indelicate remark during a board meeting. It was a failed attempt at humor. I still wish sometimes I could bite off my tongue.	I imagine that other people never commit this kind of error. That's silly. I hear people do it all the time. I'm more careful now. That's all I need to know.

Worrying

While brooding is living regretfully or resentfully in the past, worrying is living fearfully in the future. Worry is another habit of thought contrary to Attention and incompatible with a high quality of life. Frank also examined his worrying habits and then disputed them as follows:

Possible Future Events I Needlessly Worry or Dream About	Why It's Unnecessary
Worrying I will never be able to retire.	I'm doing the best I can to make a living and save money. That's all I can do.
Dreaming of owning a much faster computer.	I once bought a brand-new state-of-the-art computer. My well-being went down, not up. After spending hours learning how to use it, I wasted a lot of time in high-tech, unsatisfying activities.
Wondering if my son will turn out to be gay.	There's nothing I can do. I won't love him any less, either way.
Worrying that my occupation will become obsolete.	I already have a long list of things I can do to improve that situation. I'm doing some, and waiting for further developments. I'm already handling it well.

Is Attention Practical?

I'm often asked if social progress and personal growth would grind to a halt if everyone practiced Attention as I describe it. No, for this reason: Attention does not discard *all* value judgments, only *unnecessary* value judgments. What's the difference? If someone you care for lovingly hands you a bunch of daffodils, it is pointless to think, however secretly, *Nice, but I would have preferred roses.*

Make a list of your own favorite subjects for brooding and worrying. Try to come up with at least a brief dispute for each one.

My Favorite Worrying and Brooding Topics	Why They Are Unnecessary

But now imagine you are shopping for flowers to plant in your garden. The nurserywoman might say, "We're having a big sale on daffodil bulbs today." You might reply, "Thank you, but I really prefer roses." This does not contradict Attention. The situation is one you have some control over. Practicing Attention does not mean giving up all value judgments. That would be impossible anyway. It's human nature to make value judgments all day, every day. Practicing Attention means giving up the effort to bend the world to your will.

In the same way, if you live upstairs from a noisy bar, you have three choices. You can cultivate serenity about the noise. You can rage and curse, in utter futility. Or you can move. Let's say you can't afford to move. Attention doesn't stop you from planning to move, or from planning to make more money so you can move sooner. Still, for the moment, you're left with two choices—futile complaining, or cultivating serenity about an annoyance. Isn't the choice obvious?

Meditation and Attention

Sometimes the best of use of your mind is *not to use it at all.* At first this assertion might seem absurd. How can you not use your mind at all? The brain, of course, never stops working. By "not using your mind" I mean deliberately blurring the focus of your attention and resisting the temptation to solve any particular problem, to brood, or to worry. This is the essence of all meditation techniques, and not coincidentally, it is also a form of Attention practice. In some sense meditation is the ultimate Attention or mindfulness practice. One way to understand meditation is that you make a deal with yourself: for a period of time, perhaps twenty minutes, an hour, or for the duration of a meditation retreat, you will refrain from making any value judgments about internal or external reality; you will dwell only in the present; and you will refrain from trying to solve any problems or accomplish anything of practical value, other than the simplest tasks of daily living. It's impractical to live this way all the time, but to live this way intensely for short, carefully planned periods of time is a wonderful lesson in Attention.

Set aside fifteen minutes for the following exercise. If possible, use a timer so you won't be watching the clock. Turn off the telephone ringer and lock the door.

- Be aware of the feel and heft of this book in your hand.

- Be aware of the pressure of the chair (or whatever) against your body.

- Be aware of all the sounds around you, including the quiet ones and the miscellaneous, "unimportant" ones. Do not judge them as desirable or undesirable.

- Be aware of the smell of the room, without judging it. (Each room has its own distinctive odor.)

- Casually look around. See what you see without evaluating it.

- Be aware of the rhythm of your breath. Then be aware of your heart beating, then your digestive sensations. (These are barely perceptible.)

- Be aware of the various sensations in different parts of your body. Don't think of them as good or bad. They are what they are.

- Be aware of the tempo of your thoughts and their predominant mood. Don't try to change them. Don't try *not* to change them.

- If you are restless at first, be aware of the restlessness. Don't try to change it.

- Do nothing other than gently pay Attention to the here and now until the fifteen minutes is up.

- If you find your Attention moving into the past or the present, or to problem-solving, gently move it back to the here and now, without self-reproach. Repeat the foregoing instructions as necessary.

What happened? Whatever it was, make a record of it here for future reference.

_____

_____

_____

_____

_____

This exercise is interesting because it can be repeated numerous times with different results each time.

Attentive Habits of Thought

You've identified some habits of thought that are inconsistent with Attention and considered some of the benefits of living with greater Attention. Now you must learn to dispute nonattentive thought habits and formulate alternate thought habits that are more consistent with the principle of Attention. You can then try to make the new thoughts habitual, concentrating particularly on challenging situations.

In the following table, I've written some typical nonattentive thoughts in the left-hand column. In the center column I've disputed them, and in the right hand column I've substituted attentive thoughts applicable to the same situation.

When one lives in Attention, one lives as if the present moment is a gift. When living attentively, a bird's song may be as important as a symphony; a conversation with a store clerk or garbageman as important as a conversation with the president of the United States. When living in Attention, each one of our actions is important, each one worthy of our full respect. Genuine ugliness and despair become less common because we do not dirty neutral or potentially pleasant situations and places with ugly, despairing habits of thought.

Nonattentive Thought	Dispute	Alternate Attentive Thought
I sure wish this game of Candyland would end so I could read my newspaper.	If I were at the office, working late, I wouldn't care about the newspaper. I'd wish I could be home playing with my kid before his bedtime.	I'm going to relax and breathe deeply. I'm going to focus on the pleasure of being with my kid instead of the tedium of the game.
Ohmigod! The neighbor has painted his house Day-Glo tangerine! I can't bear it!	There's not a thing I can do about it. He won't re-paint it on my account. I'll probably get used to it.	This is what makes life interesting. You never know what's going to happen next.
If I have to watch one more beer commercial during a time-out, I think I'll just shoot myself to end the misery.	No advertisements would mean pay-TV or no televised sports at all. I'm free to ignore commercials if I want to.	I guess I'll get out the birdseed and feed the birds during the commercials. I'll be able to hear when the game starts again.
I can't stand those bad-mannered young men with their nuclear-powered boom boxes, playing that ugly, ugly music.	Unless I'm willing to murder them all, and pay the price for doing it, they are a phenome-non of nature, sort of like poison oak. I don't have to like it but I can't change it.	Maybe I'll try to get to know a few of those guys. They don't seem totally dangerous. Maybe they can explain what the lyrics say and why they like the music. That might help me get more comfortable.

Ultimately, the principle of Attention arises from deep understanding of the following:

- Our minds are disturbed not by events but by the view we take of them.

- For most people, life is what happens while they're making other plans.

- No snowflake falls in an inappropriate place.

- There's beauty and goodness just about everywhere, if you are ready to see it.

- If you *expect* to find ugliness and despair everywhere, you will.

- Wherever you go, there you are! Wishing to be somewhere else can only do harm.

- Life teems with unintended consequences; seemingly small actions often produce big results just when they're least expected. The best strategy is to perform each action with reverence and interest.

Now, you repeat the process. In the left column, enter some of your most frequent nonattentive thoughts. In the center column, dispute them as best you can. In the right column, enter some alternative habits of thought consistent with the principle of Attention that you'd like to cultivate.

Nonattentive Thought	Dispute	Alternate Attentive Thought

7

Gratitude

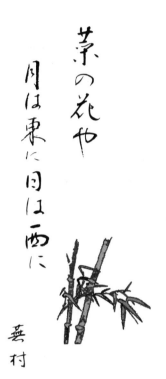

Gratitude, like Compassion and Attention, represents a habit of thinking. It also represents habitual avoidance of nongrateful thinking, particularly resentful thinking and entitlement-based thinking. Why choose Gratitude? The most important and obvious reason is that Gratitude feels good; it adds to the total of our life's joy. Grateful people are more popular, more eager and enthusiastic, perhaps more creative. Why reject resentment? Resentment feels bad. Resentful people are less likable. Resentment drains energy, enthusiasm, and creativity.

The Gratitude Game

Make a brief note of your mood—just as it is at this moment—in the following lines.

_____

_____

_____

Now, wherever you are at the moment, look around and identify, more or less at random, four or five items or circumstances. Make a list of them. Taking one item at a time, brainstorm about the reasons each object might evoke Gratitude in some way. Here's an example.

Item	Reasons for Gratitude
Clock	Silent, reliable, accurate, inexpensive, not unattractive. It makes life much more convenient. Three hundred years ago, only the richest people owned timepieces.
Tree outside window	Each tree is uniquely beautiful. It provides me with shade on hot days. It's a choir loft for birds. It makes oxygen. It makes fragrant flowers in spring.
Warm room	It's cold and rainy outside. I could survive out there, but I might not have any fun or accomplish anything other than survival. Normally, I take a warm dry room for granted, but how pleasant it is to recognize the luxury and enjoy it.
Telephone book	It's free. How lucky I am to be able to reach so many people so conveniently. If I need a product or service, finding it is almost effortless.

Now you try.

Item	Reasons for Gratitude

Now, make another brief note of your mood. If you're like most people, your mood has become more cheerful.

_____

_____

_____

I'll follow the pattern of the previous two chapters by first identifying some habitual thoughts utterly incompatible with Gratitude that are widely found among normal people.

- I deserve to be treated courteously by store clerks.

- I've paid my dues. I shouldn't have to work for such a low salary.

- It's hard to soar like an eagle while associating with a flock of turkeys.

- I've got champagne and caviar tastes in a soda pop and CheezWhiz world.

- Why can't my wife (husband) be attractive and sexy, the way wives (husbands) are supposed to be?

- I can't believe it! At the age of forty, I have to start taking blood-pressure medicine. What have I done to deserve this?

- (Sarcastically) Oh wow, another exciting sunset.

- I'm supposed to be grateful for our American freedoms. But if I skateboard on the post office grounds, I get arrested. What kind of freedom is that?

These items will give you some idea of how to understand nongrateful habits of thought. Most nongrateful thoughts fall into one or more of the following categories.

Believing that life's small and subtle pleasures are not worth bothering with.	
Hoping for as much excitement and luxury as possible, and feeling angry or disappointed if it doesn't happen.	
Feeling entitled to get the good things you crave.	
Believing you are more entitled to a happy comfortable life than others.	
Believing that you shouldn't have to suffer discomfort, disappointment, or hardship the way other people sometimes do.	
Feeling unable to get over a disappointment.	
Believing your desires are so important that you needn't be too concerned about how you satisfy them.	
Assuming that if your desires are thwarted, someone else deserves blame or retaliation.	

Review this list, and in the empty right-hand column, make a note of how often your thoughts resemble each item.

Small Pleasures

Given free choice between soda pop or champagne, I'll have the champagne, thank you. Given free choice between a BMW or a Yugo, the BMW will suit me better. Given free choice between charming friends or obnoxious friends, I'll go with charming. Preferences like these are human nature.

In spite of this, I practice Gratitude as diligently as I can. Why, then, am I not equally contented with soda pop or champagne? Few choices are completely free. I might not want to spend the money for champagne, especially good champagne. Champagne might not be offered. Maybe I'm abstaining from alcohol.

Circumstances like this change continually. The important question is this: If only soda pop is available, is it within my power to enjoy soda pop as much as I would enjoy good champagne? The answer is yes—if I cultivate my capacity for Gratitude.

On page 30, you learned that people who win large sums in lotteries end up somewhat less happy than they were before. This is particularly striking when you consider that most people who play lotteries work for low pay and are poorly educated. Why is this? They lose their ability to enjoy small pleasures. Before you win the lottery, you might get a great deal of pleasure sitting on your front stoop having cinnamon toast and coffee while reading the newspaper and watching the sun rise. After winning the lottery, the front stoop might not seem good enough anymore. You may become accustomed to fresh handmade French pastry, and cinnamon toast may not seem so good by comparison. After watching the sun rise over the Eiffel Tower and the Taj Mahal, it might not look so great rising over the MiniMart.

This is not just a theoretical problem, and it doesn't just happen to lottery winners. Middle-class Americans fall within the richest 1 percent of all the people alive on earth, and within the richest one-tenth of 1 percent of all the humans who have ever lived. In a sense, we *have* won the lottery. We don't realize it because we focus our Attention on the tiny number of people who are richer than us, so we feel poor by comparison. The same thing happens to lottery winners. The million bucks they win might only pay some billionaire's electric bill for a year.

Because we have already won the lottery, we have become insensitive to small pleasures that might have given us joy under other circumstances. The purpose of Gratitude is to fight this inclination. The circumstances of our lives constantly erode our capacity to enjoy small pleasures. The practice of Gratitude constantly rebuilds it.

Is Gratitude a Duty?

Too often we hear "grateful" in the same sentence with "should." No doubt, there are some things we "should" do: wear seat belts, recycle, pay taxes. But Gratitude is not a "should." It can't be. Gratitude not freely chosen is not Gratitude and does not confer the benefits of Gratitude.

Say you order eggs Benedict and fresh-ground custom-roasted coffee at a nice bistro. The waitress brings you hot water, a package of instant coffee, and hotcakes, explaining that the delivery truck doesn't run on Sunday mornings. When you protest, she says, "You've got perfectly good hotcakes and instant coffee. Most people in the world are hungry and would love to have it. You should be grateful for it!"

Somehow, I doubt that you will feel grateful for it. If your companions pressure you not to be grumpy, you might show outward signs of Gratitude, but they probably won't be genuine.

On the other hand, as she takes your order, the waitress might say, "We're having a bad day. The only coffee we have is instant, and the only breakfast item we have is hotcakes." Then, it's not so hard to imagine ordering the instant coffee and hotcakes and enjoying them quite a bit, especially if other circumstances such as the setting and company are good.

In the end, Gratitude is a gift you give to yourself. Feigning the appearance of Gratitude while under social pressure is only good manners or submissiveness.

For some people, Gratitude carries unwelcome connotations. Sometimes it seems to suggest obligation to someone or something. Perhaps someone has chosen to give you something good and you think you should be thankful for it. The answer to this problem is easy. Don't think of Gratitude in that way. Gratitude is a feeling, not a social obligation. Gratitude is simply a pleasant, happy feeling associated with some good thing you are attending to. Many people have an impulse to say thank you when they feel deeply grateful, and saying so may deepen their sense of Gratitude. Feel free to say it, if you like, to whomever you like. Or you can just thank the universe. If you don't feel like saying it, it certainly isn't necessary.

Gratitude Meditation

Through meditation, you can deepen and intensify your experiences of Gratitude. Choose a suitable item for Gratitude meditation. It might be a book, your child, some favorable circumstance, a happy memory, or a Ming vase, if you happen to own one. Make a note here of what the item is. For the purpose of this exercise, I'll call it your Gratitude item.

Get settled for at least ten or fifteen minutes of meditation. Arrange for quiet and privacy. A comfortable, alert posture is usually best. Your eyes may be either closed or open. Imagine that the feeling of Gratitude is a seed that, with your help, can germinate and grow rapidly in the next few minutes. When you're ready to begin, quietly and patiently ask yourself:

- What's good about my Gratitude item?

- What do I like about it?

- How does it please me?

- In what ways am I lucky to have it?

- How would I feel if I lost it?

- How many times has it given me pleasure?

Each time you ask yourself one of these questions, wait patiently in a still and receptive state of mind. Don't work at answering the questions the way you might work to solve an arithmetic problem. Let the answers come to you. In the same way, let grateful feelings come to you. Some of your reactions might be unexpected. Give up preconceptions of what is supposed to happen and honor what *does* happen instead.

If and when a feeling of Gratitude comes to you, think to yourself (or whisper, if you like) some of the following ideas.

- I feel grateful now.

- My capacity for Gratitude is deep and growing.

- I feel receptive to deeper feelings of Gratitude.

- I have so much I could be grateful for, if I choose.

Repeat the process whenever you like, but don't pressure yourself. You have the whole rest of your life to practice Gratitude: while working, driving, meditating, or even dreaming.

When you're done with your Gratitude meditation, sit quietly for a moment, gathering your thoughts. Savor the good experience you have just had. Make some notes of your experience for future reference.

Royce wrote,

I didn't know what to use for my Gratitude item at first. When my cat jumped in my lap, I thought, "She'll do." I started by just enjoying the warm weight of her in my lap, then the sensation of her breathing and purring. I thought of what a miraculous thing an animal—any animal—really is. It seemed amazing to me that two animals of very different species—a cat and a human—could understand each other and love each other. It seemed completely mysterious, and all the more precious because it is mysterious. My feeling of Gratitude grew very strong then. I could go on for pages, but this is enough to help me remember and relearn this lesson again when I need to.

The Practice of Gratitude

Gratitude is both a feeling and a practice. The *feeling* of Gratitude is pleasant, but it comes and goes. It is not voluntary. The practice of Gratitude involves identifying and questioning nongrateful thinking; disputing nongrateful thinking; developing alternative grateful thoughts; rehearsing new, grateful thoughts until they become habitual; developing new habits of speech and behavior consistent with grateful habits of thinking; and recognizing and enjoying the benefits—emotional and practical—that come from the practice of Gratitude.

8

Combining C, A, and G

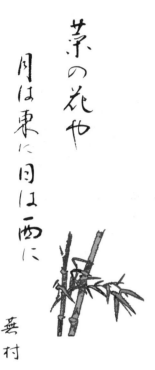

Compassion, Attention, and Gratitude are easy to understand when considered separately. That's why I discuss them separately and encourage you to study and practice them separately. The matter doesn't end there, however. Each of the three principles is related to the other two in deep and complex ways, and all three principles are connected to the world's religious, spiritual, and philosophical traditions. One could spend a happy lifetime discovering all of these connections just by reading some of the works that the teachers of these traditions have authored. Here are a few ideas to get you started.

Naturally, Christian teachings very frequently emphasize Compassion (sometimes called Christian love or charity), Attention (usually called reverence or humility), and Gratitude (usually called thankfulness). Christ encouraged these principles in many ways, and so have many subsequent Christian teachers. This is a large and complex body of literature that I do not know well, but I'd like to recommend one of my favorites, Thomas Kempis, a pious medieval monk who repeatedly restates Christian doctrine in ways that reflect Compassion, Attention, and Gratitude.

Marcus Aurelius, the Roman emperor and philosopher, might help you understand and practice the three principles. He is mainly remembered for *Meditations*, a collection of his sayings and brief essays. Rome's last non-Christian emperor, who ruled during a time of pervasive social crisis and moral deterioration, Marcus Aurelius did his best to preside in a calm, efficient, and compassionate manner with little regard for wealth, glory, or transient pleasures. He tried to record how he performed this difficult feat so that other people in other times might follow the same example. He is remembered for epigrams such as,

> *How much more grievous are the consequences of anger than the causes of it!*

and

> *When you are outraged by somebody's impudence, ask yourself at once, "Can the world exist without impudent people?" It cannot; so do not ask for impossibilities.*

The teacher and philosopher who most influenced Marcus Aurelius was Epictetus, a former slave. Epictetus' basic ideas are rather similar to those of Marcus Aurelius, but he expresses them somewhat differently, probably because of his drastically different life experience and position. Epictetus is sometimes acknowledged as the great-grandfather of cognitive psychotherapy because he said,

> *Men's minds are not disturbed by events but rather by the view they take of them.*

and

> *He is a wise man who does not grieve for the things which he has not, but rejoices for those he has.*

Reverberations of Compassion, Attention, and Gratitude can be found in a number of novels and classic works, many of which seem to me to give unintentional lessons in C, A, and G—such as what happens to people who refuse to practice the three principles.

The novelists who do this can describe flawed people in difficult situations in such a way that we love and admire the characters even when they do harm. By analogy, we learn to love our own lives and the people around us. E. M. Forster particularly affects me this way, in novels such as *Howard's End* and *A Room with a View*. Anthony Trollope's *The Warden* and its sequel *Barchester Towers* did the same. My favorite in this regard is the *Forsyte Saga* (a series of three novels) by John Galsworthy. I encourage you to seek out lessons about the three principles in these and other novels and stories.

The New Testament, through Christ's compassionate teachings, strongly emphasizes Compassion. Many Jewish and Moslem teachings also encourage charity, thankfulness, reverence, awe, wonder, and humility. These all combine C, A, and G in various ways.

Hindu and Buddhist traditions (remember that Buddha was a Hindu teacher and reformer) constantly reiterate various combinations of Compassion, Attention, and Gratitude. Buddha's third noble truth, that the renunciation of desire leads to the cessation of suffering, is a particularly direct pronouncement regarding the problem of incessant and insatiable human desires. His "eightfold path" can easily be understood as a systematic program for practicing C, A, and G.

About fifty years ago, Aldous Huxley, most famous for *Brave New World* and *The Doors of Perception*, published *The Perennial Philosophy*. Huxley believed, like others before him, that the world's great religions and spiritual traditions have taught the same underlying message. In *The Perennial Philosophy*, Huxley clarifies the underlying message and provides examples of it from Christian, Moslem, Hindu, Jewish, Buddhist, Zoroastrian, and other scriptures. According to Huxley, the perennial philosophy has three essential elements. First: ordinary things, ordinary lives, and ordinary minds are made of divine stuff. Second: a chunk of the divine Reality (Huxley's term for God or the Supreme Being) lies at the core of every living thing. Third: a person's single most important task is to discover the divinity of ordinary things, ordinary lives, and ordinary minds, and to discover her identity with the divine Reality.

I am struck by Huxley's description of the third element because it is the same as the practice of Compassion, Attention, and Gratitude. This workbook is no more or less than a simple recipe about how to begin this process of discovery.

The perennial philosophy contrasts sharply with most popular contemporary religion in that the divine Reality does not necessarily *do* anything. It is just there. It does not necessarily pluck humans out of danger nor punish others in anger. It did not necessarily create the universe, nor does it necessarily maintain the universe. Life after death is an unimportant question according to this philosophy. The essential question is whether we will ever be fully alive *before* death. Although this doctrine does not perfectly reflect the doctrine of any given religion, it fits comfortably with many.

Returning to a more practical view, consider how the three principles relate to one another. If a person diligently practices any one of the three he will eventually discover the other two.

	Gratitude	Attention	Compassion
Compassion leads to:	Greater appreciation and enjoyment of others, then to Gratitude for them then to Gratitude for other things.	Awareness of unnecessary value judgments about other people. The next logical step is to withhold needless value judgments about things, places, events, and circumstances.	
Attention leads to:	Increased receptivity to the good and beauty that are all around us.		Withholding needless judgments of people as good or bad, smart or dumb, worthy or unworthy. This in turn opens our hearts to Compassion.
Gratitude leads to:		Appreciation for insignificant and flawed things, which eventually teaches us to avoid needless value judgments.	Understand how hungry our hearts are. Then we learn to recognize and respect the hunger in the hearts of others.

Another way to investigate the deep and mysterious connections between Compassion, Attention, and Gratitude is to consider how all three are necessary for a full and satisfying life. Remove any one of them, and you have a problem.

	Without Gratitude	Without Attention	Without Compassion
Compassion	Sorrowful, bleak, and cheerless. Too much pity and too little laughter.	Too much blaming and judging in reaction to sorrow and injustice. Too little serenity.	
Attention	A dry, gritty way of life. Tedious or punctilious.		Too much self-involvement. Too little enjoyment of others or concern for them.
Gratitude		Thoughtless hedonism.	Too much self-involvement. Too little empathy.

You now know enough about the three principles and how they are practiced to consider in a more detailed way how they might improve the quality of your life. In the following chart, consider the many areas of life in which one or more of the three principles might apply. Make a check mark or a brief note of how any of the three principles might help you in any area. Don't worry about leaving cells blank. This exercise is intended only to clarify your goals and values and to inspire you to eagerly attack subsequent chapters in this workbook.

Your Goal	Compassion	Attention	Gratitude
Less worry			
Less anxiety			
More optimism			
More cheerful mood			
Less anger and hate, more forgiveness			
Better judgment			
More responsible behavior toward loved ones			
More comfortable at work			
More productive at work			
More creativity			
More honesty			
More likable, more friends			
Fewer disputes with others			
More kindness			
Deeper spiritual understanding			
Deeper Christian faith			

Deeper Jewish faith			
Deeper Hindu or Buddhist faith			
Deeper secular-humanist faith			
Deeper faith of another type			
More rigorous spiritual practice			
More satisfying meditation or prayer practice			
Happier marriage			
Better parent			
More dedicated to social justice			
More reverent and protective of the planet			
Abstinence from drugs and alcohol			
Healthier lifestyle			
Simpler lifestyle			
Other:			
Other:			
Other:			

Here's how Charlotte filled out this table. (Blank rows are deleted.)

Your Goal	Compassion	Attention	Gratitude
Less worry	Less obsession with my own small, ordinary concerns.	More serenity about difficult feelings.	Less obsession about getting ahead.
More optimism	Expect more good in people around me.	Stop blaming and condemning others so much.	
More cheerful mood			I feel happy whenever I remember to practice Gratitude.
Better judgment	More willing to accept the reality of other people's feelings and attitudes.	Maybe will get less frantic when things are not as I would like them to be.	
More responsible behavior toward loved ones	Sometimes my husband is doing the best he can, even though I'm not satisfied. I will learn to back off.		Enjoying my kids more, molding them less.
More comfortable at work		Forget about trying to remake the company to my specifications.	
More creativity	I'd like to express Compassion in my portraits.	Depend less on inspiration. Instead, take more interest in what *is*.	
Deeper spiritual understanding	Give up the idea that everybody should agree with each other about spiritual questions.		Gratitude is probably the best route to grace, but it's the one I use least.

Deeper Christian faith	Christ as "redeemer" doesn't always work for me. Christ as a great teacher of Compassion is much more comfortable.	Gratitude for a supportive Christian community.	Less judging and condemning. How presumptuous! That's God's job, not mine.
More reverent and protective of the planet	Sometimes environmental responsibility seems like a burdensome obligation. If I think of Compassion for all living things, then I'm happy to do it.		
Abstinence from drugs and alcohol		I usually drink when overcome with sad memories, and don't think about what I'm doing. Attention will help.	Feeling grateful for all the good things I could throw away by drinking.
Other: Taking care of Mom	Doing it out of pure duty is too depressing. Doing it out of compassionate love is so much nicer.	No more thinking, *Why should this be?* and getting angry.	

In the end, Compassion, Attention, and Gratitude are different roads to the same destination, like three spokes connecting to the same hub. Far from the destination, they seem to have nothing to do with each other. One might think, *What does enjoying this sunset have to do with loving my obnoxious roommate?* or *How will random acts of kindness help me manage my panic attacks better?* The three principles *do* converge at a certain point. In a very intimate love relationship, for example, Compassion, Attention, and Gratitude, in regard to the loved person, become very difficult to tell apart. When one is feeling very close to nature, it's hard to distinguish between the three principles with regard to the life forms, beauties, habitats, and mysteries all around you. Maybe the single expression that best summarizes the ultimate goal of wanting what you have is simply "loving life."

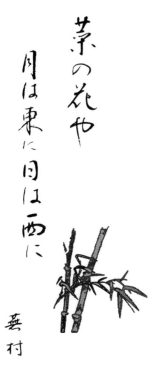

9

Depression and Grief

Discouraged? Tired? Sleeping poorly? Feel sad all the time? Feel like a total failure? When your therapist tells you you have an inferiority complex, do you worry that she is too nice to tell you that you are actually inferior? Are you surprised when people congratulate you on your perfect impression of Eeyore?

You might be depressed. What you should do depends upon how bad it is, how long it's lasted, and what kinds of symptoms you're having. Please excuse me while I shift into psychiatrist mode for the next few paragraphs.

Seriously consider seeking psychotherapy, psychiatric medicine, or both if:

- You are so depressed you can't function—you can't do the basics of your work, your social and family life, and so on.

- You are somewhat depressed and you have a history of one or more episodes of severe depression.

- You are hearing voices, having delusions, or have bizarre ideas about what an evil or worthless person you are.

- You think you might be manic-depressive (also known as bipolar mood disorder). If you have long periods of hyperactive elation and poor judgment alternating with episodes of serious depression, you could be manic-depressive.

- You have attempted suicide or you are presently considering suicide.

Even if your depression isn't that bad, antidepressant medication or psychotherapy might still be worth a try. Don't set up a false dichotomy between medication or psychotherapy on one hand and Compassion, Attention, and Gratitude on the other. You can see a therapist and take psychiatric medicine regardless of whether you practice Compassion, Attention, and Gratitude. And you can practice them regardless of whether or not you are depressed, in therapy, or taking medicine.

Handling Depression and Grief with Compassion

In one of the most famous teaching stories attributed to Buddha, he alleviates extreme grief by teaching universal Compassion.

Once a grieving mother came to the Buddha, carrying her dead baby in her arms and pleading with the Buddha to restore the child's life somehow. He said he could make a medicine to cure her suffering. In order to prepare it, he required a mustard seed from a house where none had died. She sought for long, in vain, and then returned and told him of her failure. Ironically, as a result of her experience she became able to bear her burden of grief.

The Buddha explained to his students that all living things soon die. As a result, we must all grieve at times. If we become isolated in our grief by imagining that our feelings are unique or incomprehensible to others, our suffering is multiplied. If, instead, we practice Compassion for others who suffer in the way we suffer, our burden of sorrow becomes bearable. By meeting ordinary people much like herself who had suffered as she was suffering, the mother developed Compassion for them. When her capacity for Compassion grew, she felt better, though she was likely sad.

If it feels right, attempt a milder version of Buddha's mustard-seed cure by filling out this chart and recording your experiences.

The sorrow that you suffer:

How you imagine that you suffer alone:

Who else suffers in a similar way? (If you don't know anybody who does, how could you meet others with similar trouble? If that isn't possible, imagine how others suffer like you do.)

What you learn from others whose sorrow is similar to your own:

Compassionate thoughts for others whose sorrow is similar to your own:

How does your Compassion for others in a similar situation help you bear your own burden more easily?

Record how your sad feelings changed as a result of this exercise:

Depressed people often have the sense of being completely alone, as though no one could possibly understand their feelings or sympathize with them. At the same time, they feel they have nothing to offer anyone else. For these reasons, depressed people often withdraw socially.

In the nineteenth century in Europe and North America (and probably at other times and places about which I am ignorant), it was widely believed that the best way to dispel sadness and sorrow was to find someone less fortunate than yourself and do something to assist her. These people recognized that exercising Compassion for another person often brightens up your view of the world.

Brainstorm a little about what you might be able to do for whom.

_____

_____

_____

_____

_____

Make a record of what you did and how your mood changed.

_____

_____

_____

_____

A previewer named Russ wrote the following:

I was really upset because it looked like me and my girlfriend were going to break up. I stayed in my room watching TV, drinking beer, and trying not to cry for about three days. My neighbor, a middle-aged divorced working woman with a couple of young teenagers, mentioned to me one day that her car was overheating and she was afraid of losing her job. I spent the day installing a new water pump in her car. I was sad, but I also enjoyed feelings of affection for this unfortunate woman and her two children. They were so grateful to me, I sort of began feeling lovable again. I still felt sad, during and after, but not devastated.

Handling Depression and Grief with Attention

There are two obvious and sensible ways the principle of Attention can be applied to depression.

First, depressed people tend to become preoccupied with sad memories, past hurts and disappointments, and lingering anger over past problems with others. Depressed people also tend to imagine themselves forever depressed.

Returning to the present can help. Remember, joy only happens in the present. Love only happens in the present. Bad feelings over past events are quite understandable, and within reason they are normal. But when they take over your life and make you suffer, you're living too much in the past.

Most therapists correctly discourage repression and denial. ("I'm just going to put it out of my mind.") However, choosing to live more in the present is not necessarily a form of repression. When practicing Attention, you are not violently denying your feelings, thoughts, and memories. You do not deny the existence of genuine feelings and memories, however unpleasant. You are simply redirecting your Attention to the present in a gentle, patient way.

Here is a list of strategies for living more in the present. Once you have the idea, feel free to invent more of your own. Not all of them will appeal to you, and some may be more helpful than others. Try the ones that seem most promising. Keep a record of your attempts and the results.

Activity	Result
Spend time close to nature. Don't hike strenuously. Quietly notice whatever you find around you.	
Spend time playing with a pet. Focus exclusively on the animal.	
Eat a really good meal. Focus on the good food and the pleasure of eating it.	
Have a conversation in which you primarily listen, carefully, with interest.	
Perform one household chore slowly and patiently. Do it as well as possible.	
Play with a child who enjoys your company. Focus entirely upon the child and the activity.	
Sit in meditation. Don't meditate for any preconceived purpose.	
Other:	
Other:	
Other:	

The second way that Attention can be applied to depression is by eliminating unnecessary value judgments. Depressed people make innumerable unnecessary negative value judgments about themselves. When really depressed, they make similar judgments about all their circumstances and activities. Standard psychological treatment of depression vigorously disputes those value judgments. You can do about the same thing by systematically applying the principle of Attention.

Debbie, presently suffering from moderate depression, made the following list of pointless value judgments about herself in the left-hand column of the following table. Then she went back and questioned or disputed each one.

Value Judgment	Dispute
I'm too fat.	I'm definitely too fat for magazine covers, but my husband and children, many of my relatives, and a few of my friends really do love me and will continue to love me.
I'm a loser.	"Loser" is a mean word that almost anyone can say about anyone else. I'm doing the best I can, just like everybody else. I do some things very well; I do many things fairly well.
I'm no good at sports.	Neither was Mother Teresa. So what?
I'm a bad driver.	But I've had no citations. One accident, not my fault.

The important thing about disputing value judgments in this way is that the disputes have to come from you. The benefit arises from the mental effort of formulating the disputes, and recalling them when you are assaulted by self-condemnation. If other people dispute them on your behalf, you'll probably ignore or disbelieve them. In any case, they have more impact if you make the effort to figure them out yourself.

Try making a chart similar to Debbie's.

Value Judgment	Dispute

Compassion for Yourself

Students of C, A, and G often ask about Compassion for one-self. This seems like a reasonable idea, but it does introduce complications. The essence of Compassion is the recognition that you are not the center of the universe and that other people's feelings are much like your own and arise from similar sources. Thinking this way about yourself might be confusing.

Think of Compassion for yourself as the recognition of your own humanity. You have hopes and fears just like everybody else; you have sorrows and disappointments just like everybody else; you make mistakes just like everybody else. Recognizing these things and internalizing them is really more like Attention than Compassion. Harsh unnecessary value judgments about yourself, your feelings, your hopes and fears, and your mistakes are indeed depressing. It is within your power to give these up, though you may need some practice.

Handling Depression and Grief with Gratitude

If you are depressed, you may feel that you have lost your capacity for Gratitude. You probably haven't lost it entirely, though; more likely it's just gone dormant. You can wake it up again.

Remember, Gratitude is both a feeling and a habit of thought. You might say you are depressed partly because your feelings of Gratitude are diminished. (Grateful feelings are often described as happy feelings, and this is good enough for casual use, though there are some differences.)

Loss of grateful feelings is not voluntary. You didn't push a button to turn them off, and you can't do the same to turn them back on again. Habits of thought, on the other hand, are under voluntary control; they can be altered. When depressed you will probably have to work harder at the practice of Gratitude. Your grateful feelings might come less frequently, or they might be less intense. Nevertheless, if you alter your habits of thought in accordance with the principle of Gratitude, deep feelings of Gratitude will likely come along soon enough, and more often. An excellent way to respond to depression is to spend more time cultivating Gratitude until your capacity for it gradually returns.

It's also possible that you've never been very good at Gratitude. There is no reason you can't begin cultivating it now, for the first time, even if you are depressed.

Reread the ungrateful habits of thought outlined on page 58.

Choose one of these as a habit of thought that might contribute to your depression, and write it here:

Sylvia chose "Feeling unable to get over a disappointment."

I just can't believe that our house got foreclosed and we had to move into an apartment. It's so unfair! Lots of people have less education and easier jobs than we do. Why don't they get foreclosed? I keep thinking of all the work I put into that house, decorating it and fixing little things. It was like one of my children. And the thing that really hurts is that our monthly rent is about the same as what our house payments were. I am just so disappointed and angry, I feel like I can't get any pleasure out of life. I've pretty much given up the idea that I'll ever enjoy life again.

Now expand on the ungrateful thought you identified as a problem for you:

_____

_____

_____

_____

_____

Sylvia disputed the idea that she might as well give up all hope of happiness because her home was seized by the bank:

This is a big disappointment to me, but it's not like my life has ended. Really, my life has stayed the same in most ways. My husband and I still really love each other, for example. We still take long walks together. The kids still joke and roughhouse with their Dad in the evening. We have less living space and the neighborhood isn't so nice. These are the only important things that have changed. I guess I can get used to them. When I think of a really serious illness in the family, or real poverty or something like that, our misfortune seems kind of small.

Dispute *your* depressing, ungrateful thought in the following lines:

_____

_____

_____

_____

_____

Finally, Sylvia identified some good things for which she felt able to cultivate Gratitude, and made a brief comment about each item.

Item	Comment
The sound of my children laughing	If I am open to Gratitude, the sound of my children laughing gives me pleasure. If my kids are still laughing—and they often laugh very happily—it can remind me that things are not really so bad.
Music	I've stopped listening to music. I feel too miserable to bother picking out something I might like to hear. If I take the trouble, certain music still gives me a lot of pleasure.
Dancing	If I just move my body to music, just a little, I always feel good.
Cuddling with my husband	When we got married we really believed that we didn't care about being rich or poor as long as we could be together. Really, that's still true. We've just sort of forgotten it.

Now make a list for yourself.

Item	Comment

Unpopularity and Social Isolation

Depression is a cruel illness in many ways. One of its cruelest aspects is that depressed people become less popular with their friends and relatives. At the same time, depressed people tend to withdraw socially because they feel tired and anxious about social relationships. Yet social isolation tends to make depression worse.

One of the reasons people become less popular when they are depressed is that they take little interest in the world around them, they complain, and they speak pessimistically. Eeyore, in *Winnie the Pooh,* is a perfect example. No one really dislikes Eeyore, but his friends don't normally get much pleasure from his company, either.

One way to turn this problem around is to practice Gratitude when you are in the company of others. Making sincere and grateful statements will help you develop more grateful habits of thinking. If you're going to do this, it's very important to avoid fake cheeriness and unintentional sarcasm. For instance, let's say you're invited to a company picnic. You go, reluctantly, and then it rains. You might say to your friend from the office, "I suppose we should be grateful for rain because it makes the flowers grow." That's sarcastic. It's unpleasant to listen to and may depress your friend. Another sarcastic and unpleasant comment might be, "Hey, I *like* watery coffee and soggy hamburgers. I don't see what difference the rain makes."

After a moment of careful thought, you might be able to say something more genuinely grateful, such as, "I'm really glad that after all we've been through, our coworkers and bosses still care enough about each other to plan a company picnic once a year."

Use the chart on the next page to formulate some grateful remarks you might make in the near future, in foreseeable times and places. At the same time, anticipate possible sarcastic remarks you might be tempted to make. If you anticipate them now, you'll be less likely to say them when the time comes.

Grief

By definition, grief hurts. What's worse is that the pain goes on and on, as if it will never stop.

It helps to acknowledge that grief is a normal reaction to loss. Just about all humans, in every culture and at every time in history, have experienced grief in reaction to sad losses. The psychological function of grief is still somewhat mysterious, but it appears to be essential. Grief is not just normal; it's somehow necessary.

Where, when, and to whom	Grateful things I want to say	Remarks to be avoided

This is scant comfort when the pain seems unbearable, though. Here are some ideas about how to use Compassion, Attention, and Gratitude to live through times of grief.

- Try to meet others who are grieving. You might consider offering them some kind of compassionate assistance.

- A big problem with grief is that many of the people around you don't know you are grieving. Their usual insensitivity is particularly hard to take. Others know, but manage to say all the wrong things. There is no reason your grief should prevent you from cultivating Compassion for such people. When you do, they will probably hurt you less.

- Think of your grief not as an affliction but as a tribute or memorial to the person, pet, or job you have lost.

- Try thinking of grief as a form of Gratitude. Someone (or something) good was in your life, and now he or she or it is gone. It's not hard to practice Gratitude for good things and good people from the past. Many people find grief flavored with Gratitude much easier to bear.

- Avoid unnecessary value judgments about your sad feelings. Avoid the temptation to consider sadness a sign of weakness. Sadness is sadness.

- Avoid the temptation to wonder how long you will grieve. Stay in the present.

- Notice the times when the pain stops and pleasure returns. Combine Attention and Gratitude by permitting yourself these moments of pleasure even if you know the sadness will soon return. As time passes, the episodes of sadness will become shorter and less frequent, though they'll perhaps still be intense.

10

Anxiety

The Book of Ecclesiastes (9:11) in the Bible says, "The race is not to the swift, nor the battle to the strong, neither yet bread to the wise, nor yet riches to men of understanding, nor yet favor to men of skill; but time and chance happeneth to them all."

Much as we value our health, our jobs and incomes, our good reputations, our homes, and so on, there is absolutely no way to protect them from time and chance.

The eleventh-century Tibetan Buddhist monk and teacher Milarepa put the same idea this way: "All worldly pursuits have but the one unavoidable and inevitable end, which is sorrow. Acquisitions end in dispersion; buildings in destruction; meetings in separations; births, in deaths. Knowing this, one should from the very first renounce acquisition and heaping up, and building, and meeting; and, faithful to the commands of an eminent guru, set about realizing the Truth."

Because "time and chance happeneth to us all," and because "all worldly pursuits have one unavoidable and inevitable end," anxiety is inevitable. Few people escape it. This fact seems cruel because anxiety may also be the most painful emotion. Depression aches, but anxiety cuts and stabs.

Few people stop to consider that anxiety is a very useful emotion. It helps us survive. Drugs that can wipe out anxiety (alcohol, heroin, and cocaine, for example) destroy good judgment and would do so even if they weren't addictive. A few unfortunate and dangerous people have developed little or no capacity for anxiety. Many die young. Many of the rest go to prison.

Other people are unusually susceptible to anxiety. Perhaps you meet that description. It is easy to understand how anxiety-prone people may envy others incapable of anxiety. Nonetheless, such envy is misguided.

Whether anxiety is a persistent curse or a useful tool depends upon how we manage it. A key to effective anxiety management, oddly enough, lies in being grateful for anxiety. Practicing Gratitude for the good things that we dread losing also helps. Too often we treat anxiety as if it's a disease. We try to banish anxiety by force of will or by taking medicine. When we fail to eliminate anxiety in these ways, we feel we must be weak, stupid, or otherwise personally responsible for our suffering. If you are troubled by persistent, painful anxiety, you've probably done quite a lot of self-blaming. My psychotherapy clients tell me self-blaming never relieves their anxiety. That's been my experience, too, and scientists who study these things agree.

Handling Anxiety with Gratitude

In this exercise (top of the next page), quickly run the entire videotape of your life (miraculously stored in your brain) from your earliest memories. You are scanning for situations when anxiety actually benefited you. For instance, you might have been too scared to walk a log spanning a dangerous chasm, or a fear of dogs might have prevented you from getting bitten, or a fear of talking back to an angry parent may have saved you from a serious punishment.

You may feel that anxiety has done you more harm than good. This is unlikely; after all, you have survived. It's more likely that you remember more clearly the times that anxiety got in the way or seemed to cause you needless suffering. You probably take for granted the much more frequent times that anxiety has protected you from harm or loss. Recognizing the value of anxiety will help you cope with it in the future with more poise, confidence, and good cheer.

Of course, anxiety can make us suffer and it can interfere with our plans and hopes. You may hope for relief, quite understandably.

Productive approaches to problem-anxiety are very often paradoxical. Trying hard to control anxiety seems to make it worse. Trying not to think about it makes it worse, although deciding not to take it very seriously seems to make it better. Avoiding feared situations does not alleviate the fear, even if the fear is clearly irrational—but slowly approaching a feared situation gradually diminishes anxiety. Trying not to have a panic attack often brings one about, but *trying* to have panic attacks usually prevents them.

Anxious situation	Benefit

Instead of trying hard to be strong, try some different approaches derived from the principles of Compassion, Attention, and Gratitude.

Good Things I Fear Losing

Make a list of the good things in your life you most often feel anxious about losing. Mark any of the following items that apply to you, and then add any others that occur to you.

- Losing my job
- Losing the respect of others
- Losing possessions
- Losing my life
- Losing hope for myself
- Losing my independence
- Other: _____
- Other: _____

- Abandonment by my spouse or partner
- Losing income
- Losing health
- Losing my children
- Losing hope for others
- Losing my self-respect
- Other: _____

If you are in the habit of worrying, you may associate these items with anxiety and pain. That's a little odd, if you reflect on it. After all, you still have these things now. The odds are you will not lose any of them in the foreseeable future. I once heard someone say, "My life has been a long succession of painful catastrophes, none of which has actually occurred."

Spend several minutes contemplating each item you marked. If you become aware of anxiety, put it gently aside. Instead, invite the experience of Gratitude for each item. Take time to let the feeling of Gratitude grow inside of you until it seems solid and undeniable and gives you pleasure. If you like, you can reflect, with each item, *Although I fear losing this thing, the fact is I have it now and I can enjoy it now.*

You might add, *If I lose it someday, I want to lose it only once.*

What happens to the anxiety? Here's what the previewer Alex wrote:

> *I really fear losing my job; I worry that the boss doesn't like me or my performance isn't good. As far as I know, the boss does like me and my performance is fine. I really wanted a job like this for a long time. I like the income, the prestige and respectability, the prospects. I like doing the work. I would really hate to lose it. When I think about it, I do get anxious. So, according to instructions, I gently push aside the anxiety and focus on the Gratitude instead. This is difficult, because my anxiety response has been automatic. I try remembering how badly I wanted this job when I applied for it. That helps. I try imagining how disappointed I would feel if I did lose it. That helps me remember how much I like it. I imagine myself happily getting up in the morning to go to work. Okay, now I feel the Gratitude.*
>
> *When I feel the Gratitude, my anxiety doesn't exactly disappear in a flash. Instead it sort of blends with the Gratitude and leaves me with a more comfortable feeling that seems to tell me to proceed with caution. It reminds me of borrowing my Dad's expensive binoculars as a kid. I really liked looking through them, but I dreaded dropping them. So I used them with care and with pleasure.*

Instead of thinking of anxiety as a disease or weakness, try thinking of it as too much of a good thing.

Use the following exercise to record your reflections about anxiety and Gratitude.

My fear:

The actual loss I fear:

My Gratitude for the thing I fear losing:

How my fear helps me:

Gratitude for my fear:

How my fear is too much of a good thing:

Margie offered the following:

My fear:

Afraid I won't find a job. Also fear finding a job I really hate, or that I'm not good at.

The actual loss I fear:

Financial security, respect of husband, loss of time with children.

My Gratitude for the thing I fear losing:

My husband is wonderful and supportive. I have been a stay-at-home Mom for ten years, which is something many women would love to be able to do.

How my fear helps me:

I am preparing effectively for possible new occupations, and diligently seeking the right job.

Gratitude for my fear:

Without it I am not a very ambitious person; I might postpone these tasks indefinitely.

How my fear is too much of a good thing:

When I feel sick with fear and paralyzed with anxiety, that's too much.

When you're anxious, instead of trying to be brave and strong, talk to the anxiety as if it were a person. Thank it for doing its job. Then ask it to back off a little.

For example, let's say Margie is going to a job interview. She wants the job but fears she is not qualified, and dreads that she will be ridiculed. She talks to her anxiety:

> *Thank you, anxiety, for reminding me that working to make money is one of the important things I need to be doing at this time in my life. Thank you for reminding me that my skills are rusty. Thank you for encouraging me to take job interviews seriously. You are doing your bit to help me survive. Right now, I feel like you've done a pretty good job of reminding me. I promise I'll try to remember these important things. If I forget, feel free to remind me again. Right now, you're reminding me too effectively, so I'd appreciate it if you'd back off a little. I'm so nervous I can hardly stand it.*

Fighting anxiety is like judo. You turn the force of your adversary's attack to your benefit. That's why good anxiety-management procedures are often paradoxical.

Handling Anxiety with Attention

The Tao Te Ching says water is the strongest thing on earth because it does not compete with anything or anybody. Instead, it "dwells in the lowly places that all disdain." This a poetic restatement of the principle of Attention, and it suggests a way that Attention can ease anxiety.

I've never seen this following exercise fail. I call it the Water Exercise because with it you succeed by "dwelling in the lowly places that all disdain." That is, you succeed by deliberately stewing in your own anxiety. It takes a little time and determination, but otherwise it's fairly painless. This trick isn't widely known, so few people discover it independently. Try this the next time you're having a tense, jittery day.

1. Arrange to have about an hour of quiet and privacy. Lie down on a bed or sofa.

2. Turn off music, TV, and the telephone's ringer.

3. Don't try to do anything. Don't try to sleep. Don't try to relax. Certainly don't try to plan or solve problems. Just lie still.

4. Be prepared for extreme restlessness. At first, a minute seems like an hour. You'll probably have overwhelming urges to leap off the bed to do some task that suddenly seems very important or fascinating.

5. You may feel some waves of painful anxiety. They are actually no worse than the anxiety you've been trying to run away from all day. Be passive, like a pool of water. Let the ripples of anxiety wash over you and then wash away. Sometimes peace washes over you; other times anxiety comes.

6. Plan to lie still and passive, doing nothing, for thirty to forty-five minutes.

7. After ten or fifteen minutes, you'll likely notice you feel calmer. Lying still becomes easier and more pleasant.

8. After about twenty minutes, you'll likely feel some peace.

9. After about thirty minutes, you may feel drowsy. That's a good sign. Tense, anxious people don't get drowsy. If you get very drowsy, and you have time, feel free to take a nap. Otherwise continue quietly resting and lying down until you feel relief from anxiety.

Following this procedure, consider how it reflects the principle of Attention. During your rest, you remained in the present instead of anticipating future problems. You avoided attempts to make the anxiety go away. You refrained from thinking of the anxiety as bad or undesirable because doing so is useless. Like the Tao Te Ching says, you were strong because you did not contend.

The previous exercise can be modified to make it more like meditation. It's more rigorous, but also more interesting. Instead of lying down, sit in an erect meditation posture using a chair, cushion, or meditation bench. Begin with the understanding that you will sit in meditation for at least forty minutes, even if you are uncomfortably anxious. Watch your breath, use your mantra, or do whatever you normally do in meditation.

When you feel the anxiety strongly, think to yourself, *Anxiety is just a feeling in my body. It doesn't mean I am in danger. If I let it pass, it will pass. I have been anxious before, and it has always passed.* Then continue with your meditation. You might also try observing the feelings of anxiety—the bodily sensations of anxiety—with respect and interest, making no effort to change them.

This procedure is a little like turning around and facing the bully or the boogeyman. Running away makes the fear worse. Turning around usually reveals a cowardly bully or empty darkness where the boogeyman was supposed to be.

Jackson describes the experience this way:

> *I was so scared I felt like I was going to cry, throw up, and faint all at the same time. I had made some mistakes at work. I was afraid I would be fired or my reputation would be ruined. I was afraid I would lose my whole career. I found the prospect of meditation appealing, because I hoped it would give me immediate relief from that terrible feeling. It sure didn't! It got worse. It took something like physical strength to remain seated and more or less still. I thought my head was going to explode. I wouldn't have been surprised if I had died. Every once in awhile, it would dawn on me that my experience was just a feeling. It wasn't as if anything bad were actually happening to me. The feeling of dread became more and more intense. Then, quite suddenly, without any warning or explanation, the fear just disappeared, like a bubble popping, leaving no residue. After that, my thoughts were calm. I thought, I've made a mess. I'll clean it up the best I can, and hope it works out. What else can I do?*

You may recognize the similarities between Jackson's experience and a well-known anxiety-reduction procedure called "flooding." A person terrified of rats might agree to be locked into a room densely populated with uncaged (but well-fed and disease-free) rats. For about fifteen minutes, she feels panicky.

But suddenly and effortlessly, her brain pulls the anxiety plug and her phobia is cured. Needless to say, this kind of procedure is not often employed in private practice and it isn't very popular with patients. Still, people determined to solve their anxiety problems can apply the same principles in their own lives, as Jackson did. Naturally, a certain amount of caution is advisable.

Handling Anxiety with Compassion

Many of our worst fears are social. It is not impossible that some day you will faint in a theater, vomit in a crowd, pass gas in an elevator, stammer when addressing an audience, or weep with fright on an airplane. Most people dread such incidents. Perhaps it's good that we dread such incidents a little, because the dread reminds us to proceed with caution. But some people dread such incidents so intensely that they avoid most situations where misfortunes like these might occur. Such people also feel profoundly anxious in public situations they cannot avoid. That's bad. It's also pointless. It is impossible to isolate yourself so completely that public humiliation is guaranteed not to occur.

Such fears suggest a shortage of Compassion for other humans. Specifically, they presume other humans guilty of cruelty and stupidity. With people who suffer extreme social fears, the average person on the street will never have a chance to prove himself kind, reasonable, and willing to forgive or forget.

In my experience, patients with strong social fears do take it for granted that the average stranger is a mean-spirited, dangerous brute. This is an odd form of arrogance. The presumption is, "I am civilized, peaceful, and polite, but most other people aren't."

Try this. Make a list of about twenty people you know. Choose anyone—relatives, friends, acquaintances, coworkers, and so on.

About each person, ask yourself how he or she would react to:

- an airline passenger weeping with fright

- a stranger on a city street who seems lost and distraught

- someone who vomiting in public

- someone who faints in a crowd for no apparent reason

- a stranger in a shopping mall, trembling and moaning because of a panic attack

- a nervous, stammering public speaker

- someone in an audience made to appear ridiculous by a comedian or stage hypnotist

- someone who blushes and perspires heavily because of social anxiety during a normal conversation

- a driver who pulls off the freeway in a dubious location because of a panic attack

Chances are, you'll recognize that each of the people you think of is likely to respond to someone else's social errors in a fairly civilized way. Oddly, this is true even if they are not very nice people. A terrified airline passenger or a guy vomiting in the bushes at the supermarket is just not very interesting. Even a mean-spirited person would find little reason to ridicule such people.

Every day, all day, I listen to the most intimate and private events of my clients' lives. Some kinds of incidents I hear repeatedly. I have never heard a single instance of anyone being insulted, ridiculed, badgered, arrested, or forced into a locked psychiatric hospital because of incidents like these.

If you have strong social fears, you have likely been unfair to the ordinary people who surround you as you live your life. Consider a new attitude. Presume them innocent until proven guilty.

If you like, you can make a contract with yourself (see next page).

Another way to connect anxiety with the principle of Compassion is to reread the discussion on Compassion on pages 35–44, especially these two points:

- No person's desires are any more important than anyone else's, nor any less important.

- Everybody wants approximately the same things (wealth, power, and love) for approximately the same reasons. No one ever feels they've received as much as they need and want. Everybody dreads losing the good things they have.

Anxiety has an uncompassionate element because the sufferer implicitly wishes to avoid the anguish that almost every person must suffer from time to time. The anxious person is not unkind or morally wrong in this regard, but perhaps unwise.

In order to give this insight some practical value, look at it this way. Identify a fear you'd like to reflect upon more deeply, and write it here:

_____

_____

Social Fears Contract

I, _____ , acknowledge that I have often presumed ordinary people to be cruel, rude, hostile, stupid, or dangerous. Doing so was unkind and unwise of me, and has caused me unnecessary anxiety.

In the future, I will do my best to assume that if I am distressed or embarrassed in the presence of strangers, they will take little notice, respond politely and calmly, or offer assistance, depending on the problem I present. I will also assume that they will take little notice of possible peculiarities in my appearance.

I reserve the right to cancel this contract if subsequent experience shows that ordinary people are just as cruel, rude, hostile, stupid, or dangerous as I have previously supposed them to be.

Signed: _____

Date: _____

If necessary, for the sake of clarity, identify the good thing you fear losing and write it here:

_____

_____

Jackson chose the fear of losing his job. In this case, the good thing he fears losing is income and prestige. Now consider how your fear is more or less universal.

Jackson wrote,

I guess very few people have ever had great jobs guaranteed for life. Serfs and slaves had jobs for life, but they weren't too satisfactory. Things change. Recesssions come and go. Technologies and industries change, not to mention wars, famines, and epidemics. Naturally, I want my life to be as comfortable and uncomplicated as possible. So does everybody else, to about the same degree. Is it possible that I feel I deserve a comfortable and uncomplicated life more than other people do? Is it possible that I feel I need a comfortable and uncomplicated life more than other people do? Perhaps I do feel that way. I've never thought about it.

Record your reflections on this topic here:

_____

_____

_____

_____

_____

Beginning with this line of reasoning, you might reach an obvious yet strangely unfamiliar conclusion. It goes something like this:

Of course I want to keep all the good things I already have. *Of course* I want to gain more advantages and luxuries with time. *Of course* I want to avoid death indefinitely! And, of course, so does everybody else, just as much as I do. The only option I have is to take each day as it comes, do the best I can, and see what happens. That is the only option anybody has. Of course I will have losses, just like everybody else. Some may hurt more than others. When I recognize that this is the human condition for all people and has nothing to do with me in particular, it is far less frightening.

The foregoing might seem like an exercise in shallow and comfortless logic. If so, try to use it as an affirmation instead. Read it out loud to yourself several times. Read it as if you mean it, with emotion and emphasis. If you find it helps you be less afraid, get in the habit of reflecting upon it during anxious episodes.

As I mentioned at the end of chapter 8, the ultimate goal of wanting what you have is loving life. Life, per se, contains no guarantees. It's full of chance and randomness. And life is incomprehensible without death, in the same sense that night is incomprehensible without day. One does not fully love life unless one serenely accepts its randomness and its finitude. By cultivating love of life, in all the ways discussed in this book, we can lose much of our fear of life's unforeseeable twists and turns, including death. If this seems odd or too abstract, imagine yourself after death, somehow conscious yet completely and forever outside of normal life. You might wish you could live your normal life again for one day, or even one hour. Those fears that normally torment you—loneliness, humiliation, spiders, or death—would seem as nothing compared to the joy of a few more minutes of ordinary existence.

11

Anger and
Resentment

菜の花や
月は東に日は西に

蕪村

This chapter focuses on real anger and hostility, whether or not you express it in word or deed. Not everyone needs this chapter. Do you? The self-assessment on the next page will help you decide.

I can't tell you whether your answers are above or below average, but you can find out for yourself pretty easily: identify three or four people you consider wise, likable, and happy. Ask them the same questions. How do their responses compare to yours? Perhaps you might ask them to rate you on this chart. If you are clearly angrier than they are, you might want to pay particular attention to this chapter. If your responses clearly show that you poison your life with pointless anger and resentment, this chapter might help.

Everyday anger says practically nothing about the events that seem to trigger it, but everything about the person who becomes angry. For instance, two football fans root for the same team with equal exuberance. One becomes enraged by a possible coaching error. The other laughs it off or assumes that the coach had a good reason for his decision. If the angry fan is *really* angry, he will even get angry at his friend's complacence, perhaps attributing it to weakness and stupidity.

The public is the same way. One year, everybody is upset about abuses of power by the IRS. The next year, they're angry

Question	Answer	
Do others fear your ridicule or teasing?	very few several	a few many
Do other people feel afraid of your criticism and sarcasm?	very few several	a few many
Do other people feel physically intimidated by you?	very few several	a few many
Do other people consider you hostile, resentful, or suspicious?	very few several	a few many
Do you openly criticize or blame others?	rarely often	occasionally very often
Do you find yourself rehearsing angry things you'd like to say to strangers who have caused you difficulty?	rarely often	occasionally very often
Do you brood and daydream about how you'd like to get even with certain people or groups?	rarely often	occasionally very often
Do you have angry arguments?	rarely often	occasionally very often
Do you fall asleep angry or wake up angry?	rarely often	occasionally very often
Do you use automotive maneuvers to "punish" tailgaters or slow drivers?	rarely often	occasionally very often
Do you ruminate about the stupidity of the average citizen?	rarely often	occasionally very often
Do you ruminate about the stupidity and/or dishonesty of public officials?	rarely often	occasionally very often
Do you feel outraged by minor lapses of civility in others?	rarely often	occasionally very often
Do you daydream about how to get even with someone you think has wronged you?	rarely often	occasionally very often

Do you actually go out of your way to get even with people who have wronged you?	rarely often	occasionally very often
Do you carry on angry confrontations in your imagination?	rarely often	occasionally very often

about welfare fraud. The year after that, they are angry about people who cheat on their taxes. Sexual morality that seems outrageous in one era becomes acceptable or even desirable in the next.

When you look at anger and hostility in this way, it soon becomes apparent that very little anger is justified or rational.

A Note on Assertiveness

Some temperamentally meek people are unable to confront others unless they are very angry. The anger stimulates the courage they need to overcome their fear of the confrontation. People like this might not survive at all if they didn't blow their tops now and then. This is not an ideal strategy, though. Angry confrontations put others on the defensive, which makes them stubborn or provokes retaliation. The experience is painful and perhaps embarrassing for the angry person.

The trick is to confront people, when necessary, in a calm and reasonable way *before* you become extremely angry. Assertion training helps meek people learn how to do this. Assertion training is beyond the scope of this book, but many other excellent books can help. Educational seminars and psychotherapists can also help.

Handling Anger with Compassion, Attention, and Gratitude

Anger is often involuntary. How many times have you thought, *This time I won't get angry. This time I'll just keep my cool and laugh it off?* It works sometimes, but often it doesn't. Repeated failure to control pointless anger is a rich source of comedy in television and the movies. It can be very funny to watch a character disgrace himself with a spasmodic tantrum over some insignificant matter, particularly if he has repeatedly promised himself he will say calm. But in real life, it's not funny at all. People go to prison this way. People get injured or killed. Marriages terminate. Children are abused.

Fortunately, involuntary feelings—anger as well as other feelings—can be altered and even eliminated. Simple will-power usually doesn't do the trick, though. You can't just decide to love someone you despise. The principles of Compassion, Attention, and Gratitude represent methods for indirectly controlling anger that would otherwise be involuntary.

To reduce or eliminate pointless anger, you need to prepare yourself prior to entering the situation that will anger you. This requires some ability to anticipate what will anger you. The following inventory will prepare you to do that. Then I'll move on to some specific methods, each derived from the principles of Compassion, Attention, and Gratitude.

Assess your anger-sensitivity to the following routine life events.

Item	Examples	Your sensitivity: High, medium, or low
Driving errors	Unsafe lane changes, tailgating.	
Individual stupidity	A relative often makes stupid comments about the news. A spouse can't express himself briefly or clearly.	
Defensiveness and stubbornness	A coworker refuses to discuss a safety problem that affects you.	
Honest differences of opinion	Someone disagrees with you about school bussing, the IRS, or abortions.	
Condescension and insensitivity	Your doctor speaks to you as if you were inferior.	
Honest mistakes	Your bank loses one of your deposits, causing checks to bounce. Your teenager loses the only key to the garage door.	

Rudeness and inconsideration	Strangers talk in movie theaters. Family members change the TV channel without consulting you.	
Teasing	Someone makes fun of your bald spot or tiny breasts.	
Unfair blame and criticism	The boss blames you for low production when he knows the problems are not your fault.	
Vulgarity	Someone at a party loudly recites a tasteless joke that no one wants to hear.	
Minor inconveniences	The three people ahead of you in the express checkout line have about forty items each, and all write checks.	
Individual broken promises and lies	Your husband promises to drop the film off at the drugstore, but "forgets." You knew he would. Your child tells you falsely that she has no homework.	
Anger with your children	They sometimes smart-mouth, interrupt, or contradict you.	
Vicarious anger on behalf of innocent third parties	Crime, environmental destruction, pointless wars.	
Institutional stupidity	Asinine company policies or stupid laws.	
Institutional broken promises and lies	False advertising, deceptive contracts.	
Anger with the general public	Electing a detestable candidate. Apathy about an important issue.	

Now take some time for reflection. Choose one of the items from the above list to which you are particularly anger-sensitive, and write it here: _____ .
Ask yourself some questions about it.

- How much does this form of anger benefit me?

- How much does this form of anger harm me?

- How much does this form of anger make others dislike me?

- Does this form of anger increase or diminish my quality of life?

- Does this form of anger seem to be hard on my body?

- If I could magically stop being angry about this, how would my life be different?

Record your reactions here:

_____

_____

_____

_____

_____

Charles wrote,

I chose "anger with the general public." I read the newspaper every morning and every morning I seem to end up in a rage. Millions of innocent children all over the world are dying or suffering from diseases that could be cured for a penny a person. For every inch of newspaper space they get, the president's latest peccadillo gets a hundred miles. I don't blame the journalists. I blame the public. Journalists write for their audience.

I asked myself how this kind of anger harms and benefits me and others. Obviously, it harms me. It harms my health and it sometimes spoils my enjoyment of life. Sometimes I get so worked up about it that I get cranky with the people around me. Meanwhile, my anger does nothing to solve the problem. I don't even know that the problem has a solution! This is not the only thing I get mad about; it's one of many. The same comments would apply to most of the other items on my anger list. The more I think about this, the more I regret my angry tendencies.

People often remind me that some anger seems justified or even necessary. I am asked what good it does to be compassionate toward violent psychopaths who will remain dangerous to innocent others until they are killed or locked up for life. These concerns are so deep and widespread that I must address them before proceeding with a discussion of Compassion.

Anger is *sometimes* a useful emotion. It obviously has survival value for humans and many other animal species. My concern here is about all the times that your anger does more harm than good.

Whether anger is justified or not is a pointless question. If you feel angry, your anger feels justified. Feeling justified is part of the experience of anger. No doubt the chipmunk feels justified when he chatters angrily at the dog, and the dog feels justified when he angrily chases another dog off of his territory.

The essential question is this: why should we bother to practice Compassion toward evil people?

Some religious people or idealistic secular humanists believe that our enemies can be transformed into decent, fair-minded people by the power of our Compassion. I don't believe that, though it seems a very pleasant idea. I'm more inclined to answer the question this way: frequent and intense anger harms my health, my judgment, and the quality of my life. It also tends to sour my relations with the people around me, even if I am not really mad at them. Hatred, which is only deliberately prolonged anger, does the same thing. Additionally, if I am frequently angry at a few notorious people who I've never met and who may even be dead, I will get into the *habit* of being angry or hating. This habit too often grows out of control. Look at all the angry, hateful people around you. If I want to see the world as a more civilized and loving place, the best single thing I can do is set a good example. I will of course occasionally feel angry. This is involuntary. Whether I express it and how I express it is a matter of judgment. How long and how intensely I feel anger will depend upon my habits of thought.

Do some people *deserve* our anger? If the anger benefits no one and harms ourselves, what's the point? If most Americans are angry with Timothy McVeigh or Saddam Hussein, how does that make the world a better place? How does it undo the harm that they have done? Does hating them make Americans wiser or more decent people? Despising Adolf Hitler, Joseph McCarthy, or the Salem witch-burners is even more pointless. They are dead.

So how can compassionate habits of thought alter anger and hostility? This exercise will show you what happens when you practice Compassion when you're angry. Start by making a partial inventory of the people who often anger you. These would include people you really dislike, people you resent, and people you hate. Stick with people you are actually acquainted with. Historical figures and public figures require Compassion also, but they present special problems.

Write your list here.

_____

_____

_____

_____

_____

_____

_____

Now choose one person from your list. Put a check mark by that person's name. Reflect upon the habitual thoughts that stir up your anger about this person. (Consider rage, hatred, irritation, envy, hostility, and other such feelings to be variations of anger.) Focus particularly on your uncompassionate thoughts about this person but, when in doubt, don't worry too much about whether an angry habit of thinking is specifically uncompassionate.

Veronica chose a coworker named John from her list. She wrote,

> John and I have worked in the same office for fifteen years. It's a pretty small office, so even though we don't talk all that often, we have gotten to know each other pretty well. There's no way to avoid each other! John doesn't mean to be difficult or unkind. As far as I can tell, he's an easygoing, good-natured man. Yet he rarely even bothers to say hello to me. He seems to avoid conversation with me. Every day at precisely 12:10 I see him leave for lunch. He never asks me to accompany him, even if we are leaving by the same door at the same time. He sometimes converses affably, but only if I initiate the conversation. Other times, if I attempt to initiate conversation, he seems annoyed and impatient, like his time is so important that he can't afford to waste a

couple of minutes per month chatting with me. If I had to wait for him to initiate conversation with me, I'd have to wait forever. It's all the more irritating because he makes quite a bit more money than I do, and has more professional prestige. I honestly don't know if he'd bother to tell me that the building was on fire. Well, I'm exaggerating a little, maybe. I spend half the time wondering what I have done to offend him, and the other half of the time feeling angry at him for being so aloof and selfish.

Veronica summarized her angry, uncompassionate habitual thoughts about John in the left-hand column of the following chart. In the center column, she disputed these usual angry and uncompassionate thoughts habits of thought. In the right-hand column she developed new thoughts that she intends to make into new habits.

Angry thoughts about John	Reconsideration	New compassionate beliefs
He must think he's better than other people. I'd like to teach him a lesson to the contrary.	He never says anything haughty or arrogant. He never argues. He's just silent and private.	I think he's just a quiet, soft-spoken guy who doesn't like to chat a lot. If I don't like that, it's my problem.
Someone should tell him how selfish and insensitive he is.	I doubt that he appears selfish and insensitive on purpose. I doubt that he'll ever change. What's the point of being mad?	Same as above.
I feel sorry for his wife and family. What a lump on a stump he is.	This is just meanness on my part. His wife seems to love him. His children don't seem angry at him. I'm just feeding the flames of my anger with this kind of thinking.	I hope he and his family are a good match. I hope they appreciate his many good qualities, and he theirs.
He is passive, secretive, boring, and dull-witted. He seems incapable of normal chitchat. What a chump!	He is entitled to be silent, slow-paced, and somewhat private if he wants to be.	He normally gives an honest answer to an honest question. He's not really trying to manipulate or deceive anyone. This is admirable.

He has no right to be so aloof.	He probably feels he wants to get his work done and go home. He might be preoccupied with troubles I don't know about.	He has as much right to his personality features as I do to mine.
His reputation as a nice guy is entirely undeserved.	He's not my cup of tea, but that doesn't make him an evil person.	Well, he is a benign person, without doubt. There is no malice in his aloofness.
He is unfairly rejecting me. I've been nice to him. I've done him favors. This isn't fair!	If I asked him for a favor, he'd probably do it. He has never actually been rude to me.	Here I am, disliking him, and then feeling mad because I think he might dislike me. How silly! In any case, he is not obligated to like me.

After completing this exercise, Veronica wrote,

Well, I feel better. I feel a lot less angry, but a little sad. I wish people could be warmer and more generous and trusting with each other. But then, that's just my personality. People like John probably feel overwhelmed by too much social contact. Maybe he's cautious, too. Trying to stay out of office politics, or something. They do go on here, of course. I'm no longer annoyed when he walks past me in the hall without stopping to chit-chat. Instead, I find myself thinking, "That's John, that's his personality, that's his fate. Good luck, John." I remember that he is a very decent and honest man who does his work as well as possible.

Now, repeat the same sequence as Veronica, using one of the anger-provoking people you previously identified. In the left-hand column, record some of your angry thoughts about this person. In the center column, note some of the ways you can question these angry thoughts. In the right-hand column, record more compassionate thoughts. Repeat the process as necessary for other people with whom you are angry.

Angry thoughts about	Reconsideration	New compassionate beliefs

Use this space to record how your feelings about this person changed.

Practicing Attention When Angry

"This should not be!" This is a fundamental habit of nonattentive, pointless, and useless thought. It is also a fundamental habit of angry thought.

If an innocent person is being victimized, I might take aggressive action to stop it. Yet, I need not think, *This should not be!* It is sufficient to think, *I will help this person if I can.*

If I become aware of a social problem that I believe can and should be solved, I might take strong action. I might try to convince others that it can and should be solved. I might use strong words. But I would not think that it should not be.

If I learn that someone has lied to me about something important, I might conclude that that person cannot be trusted. I might expect an apology, and might not associate with that person until I get one, but I won't think that it should not be.

This should not be! is an expression of moral outrage. Moral outrage sometimes appears admirable. It might sometimes be exploited for political purposes; it might spice up an otherwise dull speech or political campaign. Yet in the end, I believe that moral outrage is pointless and often harmful. Some people who opposed the Vietnam war were so morally outraged that they risked hand-to-hand combat with police in antiwar demonstrations. This was considered admirable among their comrades. Yet the same kind of outrage stimulates some people to bomb abortion clinics. Moral outrage, genuine though misguided, causes Israelis to attack Palestinians, and Palestinians to attack Israelis. Other examples abound in Northern Ireland, Africa, Bosnia, and elsewhere. When morally outraged people with opposing beliefs collide, the consequences are not pretty. Moral outrage is stimulating in the short run, but fatiguing and demoralizing in the long run, I've found. Once you begin a list of things that "should not be," you will never finish it. There have always been injustices, wars, criminal violence, and other equally sad and unfortunate events, and none of these things will likely disappear within our lifetimes. We should not be complacent. But neither should we be outraged.

If you find some problem that disturbs you deeply, you might work very hard to correct the problem by doing all you can to make it better. If you fail to correct it, you will be able to tell yourself that you did everything you could to help, but did not succeed. This is sad, but perhaps not devastating.

But these are extreme and hypothetical concerns. Most of the time, the types of problems that make people think *This should not be!* involve relatively mild annoyances such as litterbugs, rude neighbors, disappointing relatives, or unpleasant working conditions. You may turn these annoyances into serious problems, at least in your own thoughts and feelings. By practicing Attention, you reverse the sequence of events. You reconsider problems you have previously labeled "unacceptable." Some turn out to be mere annoyances after all. As a result, the world begins to appear to be a more pleasant place and you become a more pleasant person.

Try keeping a log of all the small things that anger you for the next few days. Be honest. When you discover how stupid most of them are, you might not want to admit them.

Anger-Provoking Incidents

When and where	Incident	Angry thoughts

If you're like most people, you'll find that most of your angry thoughts are along the lines of Charles':

- *I shouldn't have to put up with this.*

- *That person has no right to . . .*

- *I'm sick and tired of having to . . .*

- *Nobody should be able to get away with . . .*

- *I'd like to teach that guy a lesson.*

- *I've got a good mind to tell her what I think of her.*

- *Why does Darlene always have to be so annoying? I can't stand it.*

- *The stupidity of that public official is intolerable!*

The alternatives Charles came up with were somewhat repetitive, and yours probably will be too. (That's okay. Acquiring any new skill takes repetition.)

Charles wrote,

> There is no way to eliminate or avoid all the litterbugs, rude salesclerks, bad drivers, inconsiderate neighbors, oafish acquaintances, pooping dogs, demanding relatives, lousy voice mail systems, and unanswered technical-support telephone numbers. These are phenomena of nature, and not nearly so outrageous as I imagine them. For that matter, I have at times been an inconsiderate neighbor and my voice mail system also often inconveniences people. I have two choices. I can take these things and others like them with a smile, or I can spend the rest of my life angry about them.

Try making the following contract with yourself:

Anger and Irritation Contract

I, _____ , acknowledge it is very unlikely that I will ever be able to avoid the following nuisances, irritations, and frustrations, and others like them. I list the eight that most often annoy me, but my contract with myself is not limited to these items.

_____   _____

_____   _____

_____   _____

In accordance with this newly won understanding, I will do my best to accept such instances with either humor, calm serenity, sad serenity, or constructive efforts to improve the situation according to my best judgment and the opportunities available to me at the time.

Signed: _____

Date: _____

Handling Resentment with Gratitude

Resentment is a seemingly petty yet potent emotion that dominates the lives of many people, and which none of us can completely avoid. However, it can be tempered by Gratitude.

Resentment lies halfway between anger and envy. When I am resentful, typically someone has something that I want. I don't feel the other person deserves it; I believe I do deserve it. But I don't have it, and I don't have any way of getting it.

For instance, let's say my girlfriend broke up with me, though I didn't want to lose her. She's now going with another guy. I believe she is going with the other guy because he told her lies about me and made false promises to her. But she doesn't want to talk to me about it. She seems committed to the other guy. I resent him.

Life is full of disappointments, and the good things are divided up unevenly. What rightfully belongs to whom is often debatable. Does my car rightfully belong to me, or would it be more fair to share it with other people who can't afford a car, perhaps through no fault of their own? I might have one opinion. An illiterate, unemployed car thief might have another. Do Brazilians have the right to burn down their rain forests if they want to? Resentment is an inevitable outcome of the universal human desire for more, as discussed in chapter 4.

Because of the human situation, constant feelings of resentment are almost inevitable unless you make a deliberate and continuing effort to practice Gratitude. For every thing you resent, there are a hundred things you do have that you could be grateful for, but aren't.

Here's a simple and effective way to deal with resentment. Take an inventory of those things you most often resent. To do this, you may need to carry a notebook around with you. You may not recall clearly how many times you feel resentful every day, or what you resent. Resentment is a side of ourselves we prefer not to see. Once you know what you most often resent, you can prepare the antidote, in advance, through mental rehearsal.

On page 64, I quoted Marcus Aurelius, who wrote, "When you are outraged by somebody's impudence, ask yourself at once, 'Can the world exist without impudent people?' It cannot; so do not ask for impossibilities." I might add that the world could not exist without stupid people, incompetent people, cruel people, or well-intentioned misguided people, either. These are mainly the people who anger us. Knowing that they will always be with us, and cultivating serenity on that point, can free us, and them, of anger's curse—at least some of the time. Of course, there might be some planet inhabited by intelligent beings who know no impudence, incompetence, and so on. But it would not be our planet. We would be lonely there. Perhaps we would be so strange that we would make the inhabitants very angry. Better to love life, such as it is, here on earth.

In the following table, record your most frequent resentful thoughts in the left-hand column. Write a grateful idea to counteract the resentment item in the right-hand column. It'll be easier to remember if it has some logical relationship with the resentment, but that isn't essential. Almost any genuine emotion of Gratitude will counteract a wide range of resentments.

When I resent:	I will remember to be Grateful for:

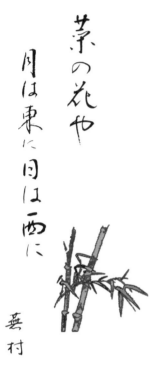

菜
の
花
や

月
は
東
に
日
は
西
に

蕪
村

12

Guilt and Self-Hate

Most of us suffer guilt and self-hate from time to time. People who never feel guilt or self-hate seem also to lack the capacity for love, loyalty, and honesty. Such people have tragic lives and often harm innocent others, including those who love them. Accordingly, within reason, we might be grateful for feelings of guilt and self-hate.

Yet guilt and self-hate, like other feelings, sometimes do more harm than good. When these feelings are intense and prolonged, they are unbearably painful. Suicides sometimes occur because people simply cannot endure these feelings any longer. Many people, at some time in their lives, will suffer an episode of terrible guilt or self-hate, perhaps for no obvious reason. A few unfortunate people waste much of their lives suffering this way. If you are going through a time in your life when you are tortured by guilt or self-hate that seems to do no good and threatens to go on indefinitely, this chapter may be useful. It may also be helpful if you have been tormented by feelings of guilt and self-hate for a long time, perhaps most of your life.

A good way to start is with a self-assessment. The next two self-assessments will form the basis for the rest of your work in this chapter.

For the sake of clarity, I'll assess guilt and self-hate separately, though they are related feelings. Guilt usually involves remorse for doing something you feel you shouldn't have done. (Sometimes it's failing to do something you think you should have done. This is called an error of omission.) Self-hate usually involves bad personal qualities you feel you possess, or good personal qualities you feel you lack.

Now that you know what the problem is, you can begin to work with it. Be as patient, brave, and hopeful as you can. The following exercises may be disturbing or painful. If you become quite agitated, take a break for a few days and return when you feel calmer.

Handling Guilt with Compassion

Do you wonder about Compassion for yourself? People most likely to ask about this generally have a lot of trouble with guilt and self-hate.

We practice Compassion for other people and other living things, but not for ourselves. We practice Compassion whether or not the other person knows of our Compassion, or appreciates it, or benefits from it. We practice Compassion indiscriminately. Naturally, if we practice Compassion diligently, others will sometimes benefit. We may forgive instead of carrying a grudge. We may smile and make a joke instead of criticizing. Compassion might even inspire some profoundly generous or heroic actions. Some people believe that Compassion for others might confer invisible, supernatural benefits to themselves as well as others. For instance, most Christians think that Compassion might help them get into heaven.

Although you direct your Compassion toward others, you are the person who benefits most from your Compassion. By blaming and criticizing less, hating less, forgiving more, and laughing and smiling more, the quality of your life improves. On the whole, this improves the quality of life for the other people around you, but that happens in a way that is often hard to perceive, partly because the effect is inconsistent and unpredictable. It would not be wise to expect others to appreciate you for your Compassion. Most people will be too busy with their own concerns to notice.

By practicing Compassion for others, you get into the habit of compassionate thinking. Accordingly, you will blame and criticize *yourself* less, and you will laugh and smile more easily at your own mistakes. You will hate yourself less, or stop that altogether, if hating yourself is normally a problem. In short, by practicing Compassion toward others you learn to be Compassionate toward yourself.

It's lucky that we benefit from practicing Compassion. If we depended upon obvious signs that our Compassion was benefiting others, we would become discouraged and perhaps stop practicing it altogether. If Compassion were strictly a

In the left-hand column of the table below, make a list of the things you feel most guilty for doing or failing to do. Don't think too hard. Just jot them down as they come to you.

Guilt Inventory

Item	Intensity	How long

Now, go back and note in the second column the intensity of the guilt you feel about each item. Use your own terms, such as "Very Strong," "Pretty Strong," "Not Too Strong," or "Just a Little." At the same time, in the far left column, note about how long (in years, perhaps) you've been feeling guilty about each item.

Now repeat the process for self-hate. In the left-hand column of the next table, make a list of the list of personal qualities you hate yourself for or can't forgive yourself for lacking. Once again, don't think too hard. Just jot them down as they come to you, then fill out the "Intensity" and "How long" columns.

Self-Hate Inventory

Item	Intensity	How long

matter of self-denial and personal discipline, few people would bother to practice it and this world would be unlivable.

Ironically, if you practiced Compassion only for your own benefit, it wouldn't work. Compassion's essential feature is that it removes you from the center of the universe. It acknowledges that everybody wants about the same things as you, for about the same reasons. It acknowledges that no one, including yourself, is particularly entitled to satisfaction of her desires; no one, including yourself, particularly deserves to suffer.

There's an old joke about narcissists. (Narcissus was the Greek god who fell in love with his own reflection. Narcissists are pathologically self-centered.) Q: How many narcissists does it take to change a light bulb? A: Only one. He hangs onto it and the world revolves around him.

Because we tend to dislike narcissists, we forget how unfortunate they are. The center of the universe is an undesirable address, because the importance of our own desires and sorrows becomes too great. Losses, disappointments, and humiliations take on monstrous proportions. By compassionately understanding the narcissist's problem, we become less narcissistic ourselves. Compassion might be understood as counternarcissism.

The exercise at the top of the next page evokes Compassion for others in such a way that you feel yourself moving out of the center of the universe, and accordingly feel more comfortable with yourself. Fill in the blank with a person or animal who would normally evoke Compassion in you. For example, you might mention your mother, a child, a victim of some injustice you detest, your neighbor's dog, or even a fictitious character such as Bambi or Thumper.

Adelaide completed this exercise in the following way:

One of the reasons I hate myself is: because I never get my house clean and my bills are often overdue. If one of the neighbor children had this same quality, my compassionate thoughts would be that nobody is perfect and everybody is good at some things and bad at others. These thoughts would probably evoke gentle laughter. I hope to cultivate more gentle laughter about myself.

Handling Guilt with Attention

You will need a quiet, private place for this exercise. Sit in a comfortable or meditative posture, and return to your inventories on page 119. Repeat the procedure beginning on the lower part of the next page for each item. (Note: this exercise will take two or three minutes per item. If you have many intense items, break this exercise down into several parts, each lasting no more than twenty minutes. Rest at least an hour or two between sessions.)

One of the reasons I hate myself is: _____

If _____ had this same quality, I would not condemn, nor would I feel hatred. My Compassionate thoughts would be:

_____

These compassionate thoughts would probably evoke the following feelings:

_____

_____

By reflecting deeply upon this example, I can begin criticizing and hating myself less.

- For each item, say something like this out loud (use a quiet, conversational tone or a whisper, as appropriate to your situation): "I have been feeling [intensity] self hate/guilt about [reason] for [duration]. Good or bad, right or wrong, this has been a fact of my life." For example, "I have been feeling pretty strong self-hate about not completing my college education, for about ten years. Good or bad, right or wrong, this has been a fact of my life." Say this phrase in a kind but matter-of-fact voice. Use a light touch with yourself.

- Ask yourself if you really heard what you said and felt the truth of it. If you didn't, repeat it once or twice, slowly and contemplatively.

- Ask yourself, "Am I ready to start feeling something else about [reason]?" For example, "Am I ready to start feeling something instead of self-hate about not finishing college?" Make a mental note of your internal answer. You might find yourself saying your answer out loud.

- Ask yourself, "Would anybody be worse off if I started feeling something else about [reason]?" For example, "Would anybody be worse off if I started feeling something other than self-hate for not finishing college?" For a minute or two, sit quietly and patiently, listening for an internal response.

- Ask yourself, "If I could start feeling something other than self-hate [or guilt] about [situation], what might that other feeling be?" For example, "If I could start feeling something other than self-hate for not finishing college, what might I feel instead . . . acceptance, serenity, forgiveness, ambition, anger, or sadness?" For a minute or two, sit quietly and patiently, listening for an internal response.

- For future reference, record the thoughts and feelings that arose in the course of this exercise:

_____

_____

_____

_____

_____

Angela made the following notes after several sessions of this exercise:

The guilt I struggled with most is about my mother. For complicated family reasons, she lives in a nursing home far away. It is difficult for me to travel there, and I can't afford to very often, but I constantly feel horribly guilty about not visiting more often. I'm usually working hard not to feel guilty, but I feel guilty anyway. At first, turning around and just facing the guilt seemed impossible—too painful. It was quite painful for about five minutes. Then something just let down inside of me. I thought, When my life is over, I will just look St. Peter straight in the eye, and tell him I did the best I could. After that, it didn't seem like such a big issue. When the guilt flares up, I just picture myself looking St. Peter in the eye, and I'm okay again, more or less.

This exercise is a good example of how the principle of Attention can become a gentle but sophisticated problem-solving tool. Trying too hard to solve a problem can make it worse. When you patiently and gently see the problem exactly as it is, without making any immediate effort to change it, you will sometimes find that the problem seems to move forward all by itself. I use the term "move forward" because problems don't often suddenly disappear. If self-hate or guilt moves into sadness or ambition, that's probably a step in the right direction. A problem that has seemed stuck for years may begin to seem less stuck.

Unnecessary Value Judgments

People often hang onto self-hate because they imagine that self-hate will somehow, some day, help them be the kind of people they want to be. For instance, someone who feels bad because she didn't finish college might imagine that if she hates herself intensely enough, she will eventually complete her college education. Conversely, she may imagine that if she stops hating herself, she will never return to college.

This kind of self-hate is a perfect example of an unnecessary value judgment as discussed under the principle of Attention in chapter 6. A value judgment that benefits no one but does do harm is certainly unnecessary. A value judgment that is obviously cruel is also unnecessary. Certain forms of guilt may also represent unnecessary value judgments, for example, feeling guilty about having survived a tragedy in which other people were killed.

See if you can reconsider some of your guilt or self-hate items in the following format.

For [how long] _____ , I have felt guilty / hated myself about

[fill in item] _____

because I thought it might help me in the following way:

_____

I know this kind of guilt or self-hate is not helpful because:

_____

For [how long] _____ , I have felt guilty/hated myself about

[fill in item] _____

because I thought it might help me in the following way:

_____

I know this kind of guilt or self-hate is not helpful because:

_____

_____

For [how long] _____ , I have felt guilty/hated myself about

[fill in item] _____

because I thought it might help me in the following way:

_____

I know this kind of guilt or self-hate is not helpful because:

_____

_____

Jonathan responded this way:

For eleven years I have hated myself for getting Sheila pregnant when she was so young, because I thought it might help me be a better father to Leilani. I know this kind of guilt or self-hate is not helpful because I love Leilani. I do the best I can for her, and always will.

Handling Guilt with Gratitude

Odd as it may seem, guilt sometimes confers benefits on yourself and others, if it is not too intense or painful. (This happens less often with self-hate.) When you fight with guilt, or become agitated about it, it can take on monstrous proportions. Guilt might be at least potentially helpful in some of the following ways.

- It reminds you not to repeat a certain mistake.

- It reminds you to resist a certain temptation that has caused you trouble in the past.

- It reminds you that you should make amends, apologize, or admit fault to someone.

- It reminds you that you have made a promise you have not kept.

- It reminds you that you are not living up to your own moral standards.

- It reminds you that you are not living up to someone else's standards.

In all but the last case, it's possible that you could benefit by giving in to the guilt, that is, by appreciating the guilt instead of feeling defensive about it or trying to justify yourself.

In the last case, failing to live up to someone else's standards, the guilt may usefully remind you that it is time to let someone know that you don't want to live up to her standards, or that you honestly don't feel able to do so.

So guilt isn't necessarily a problem; it can sometimes be a solution to a problem. If you have a tendency to shoplift, for example, you might feel guilty when you feel a desire to do it. The guilt may help you remember the many painful consequences of shoplifting, and may also help you remember that you honestly believe shoplifting is wrong. Guilt becomes a problem when it turns into self-hate. Self-hate is hardly ever helpful. One way to prevent guilt from turning into self-hate is by respecting moderate guilty feelings and being thankful for them.

Some of your guilt items can probably be restated in the format on the next page. Fill in the blanks with your own guilt items, if any apply.

Adelaide responded this way:

If my guilt about using a lot of drugs when I was a teenager is not too intense, it can actually help me by reminding me to consume marijuana and alcohol in moderation when I feel like overdoing it. I can be thankful for this form of guilt, with no need to hate myself.

Self-hate often represents unrecognized greed or envy that has grown out of control. To wish to be attractive is perfectly natural. The same goes for wishing to be intelligent, athletic, youthful, slender, charming, prosperous, well-educated, well-dressed, successful, influential, happily married, and satisfyingly employed. Yet very few people in this world can hope to be above average on all these qualities. (Mathematically inclined readers will see that only one person out of eight thousand will be above average in all of these areas, assuming they are uncorrelated.)

If my guilt about [fill in item] _____

is not too intense, it can actually help me by reminding me [to/not to]

_____

I can be thankful for this form of guilt, with no need to hate myself.

If my guilt about [fill in item] _____

is not too intense, it can actually help me by reminding me [to/not to]

_____

I can be thankful for this form of guilt, with no need to hate myself.

If my guilt about [fill in item] _____

is not too intense, it can actually help me by reminding me [to/not to]

_____

I can be thankful for this form of guilt, with no need to hate myself.

It is natural to want all these desirable qualities, but very, very few people possess all of them. Some people develop the unfortunate habit of being angry or resentful because there is some desirable personal quality they do not possess and may never possess. They may envy or resent others who have a desirable quality they lack, and may also blame themselves unfairly for failing to be extraordinary people.

Try rating yourself on each of the following desirable personal qualities:

Healthy	above average / about average / below average
Attractive face	above average / about average / below average
Attractive figure	above average / about average / below average
Athletic	above average / about average / below average
Intelligent	above average / about average / below average
Well-educated	above average / about average / below average
Influential	above average / about average / below average
Prosperous	above average / about average / below average
Youthful	above average / about average / below average
Well-dressed	above average / about average / below average
Charming	above average / about average / below average
Happily mated	above average / about average / below average
Happily employed	above average / about average / below average
Satisfaction with children	above average / about average / below average
Special talents	above average / about average / below average

Most people will be above average in a few categories, average in most, and below average in a few. Contrary to intuition, being above average in most categories is no guarantee of happiness, and being below average in most categories does not necessarily cause unhappiness. Your expectations are more important than the actual facts of your situation. If you suffer from self-hate, chances are you hate yourself for falling below average in some of these categories.

Alfonso responded in this way:

Healthy	above average / <u>about average</u> / below average
Attractive face	above average / about average / <u>below average</u>
Attractive figure	<u>above average</u> / about average / below average
Athletic	<u>above average</u> / about average / below average
Intelligent	above average / <u>about average</u> / below average
Well-educated	above average / <u>about average</u> / below average
Influential	above average / about average / <u>below average</u>
Prosperous	<u>above average</u> / about average / below average
Youthful	above average / about average / <u>below average</u>
Well-dressed	above average / <u>about average</u> / below average
Charming	<u>above average</u> / about average / below average
Happily mated	above average / <u>about average</u> / below average
Happily employed	<u>above average</u> / about average / below average
Satisfaction with children	above average / about average / <u>below average</u>
Special talents	above average / about average / <u>below average</u>

Alfonso has many desirable qualities. He is above average in five categories and average in five more. Unfortunately, he is inclined to self-hate. He has hated himself for many years because he has not achieved outstanding success in any area of life, because his face is not handsome, and because he does not have any special talents. (He wishes he could play the piano, for example.) When he feels bad, he thinks, *I am just an ugly, boring failure.* When the mood gets strong, he even hates himself for his desirable features. Then he thinks his charm just means he's shallow and his prosperity demonstrates nothing but dumb luck.

In essence, Alfonso feels entitled to be above average in almost every category and below average in practically none. It seems unfair to him that he should have a funny face, an undistinguished career, and an inability to play the piano. This is not to say that Alfonso is a bad person, or even an unpleasant person. He might be very decent and kind, and he admits he is charming. His sense of entitlement mostly hurts himself.

Grateful habits of thought are a specific antidote for entitlement and, consequently, they often help with self-hate. If Alfonso could cultivate Gratitude for his many good qualities, combined with the successes he has achieved and the comfortable life he is able to live, he might not be very concerned about his funny face and lack of musical ability.

Consider the following contract you could make with yourself. Don't fill it out immediately. Work out some possibilities on a piece of scratch paper until you develop the combination you like.

Self-Hate Contract

When I begin to hate myself for [fill in the blank] _____

I will remember to recall the following good qualities and lucky circumstances I actually possess:

_____

_____

_____

I will reflect upon these good qualities until I actually feel Gratitude in my bones, in my heart, and in my soul. I will reflect upon them until I feel thankful instead of envious, and serene instead of angry.

Signed: _____

Date: _____

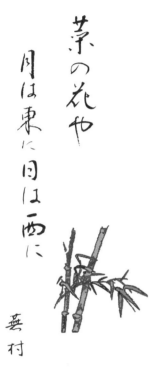

13

Optimism and Pessimism

Are you an optimist or a pessimist?

When the phone rings unexpectedly, do you expect good news or bad? When you expect a house guest, do you anticipate good companionship, laughter, and love, or inconvenience, headaches, and inconsideration? When you find out that an elected official has misbehaved, do you thank God we live in the kind of country where rascals can be voted out of office, or assume that all the other elected officials got away with similar misbehavior? If your spouse is out late and you don't know where he is, do you assume he is having a good time and will come home full of love and good cheer, or assume he is out doing selfish and disloyal things?

Optimism and pessimism are not easy to define precisely. Most people have a vague notion that optimists expect good things to happen to them whereas pessimists expect bad things. That's a fair start, but the matter goes quite a bit deeper.

Imagine that you are out for a walk on a pleasant sunny day. When you are a mile or two from home, a cool wind arises and the sky begins to cloud. You continue on your walk, unconcerned. The sky begins to look a little stormy. A few small drops of rain spatter on the sidewalk. You try to recall the weather forecast, but can't. Suddenly you feel ill and disoriented. You feel very sleepy. You are in a hospital. Some-one with a stethoscope and a clipboard is telling you you were struck by lightning yesterday. You have a broken leg, some second-degree burns, and your eyebrows may never grow back. Otherwise you're fine, and will probably recover fully.

An optimist would say, "I must be the luckiest guy who ever lived! I get struck by lightning and what happens to me? Practically nothing! I get a month of paid sick leave from work while my busted leg heals. I basically get paid for reading all the books I've wanted to read for a long time. I lose those ugly bushy eyebrows. I lose weight on the hospital diet. And now, here I am, six weeks later, alive to tell the tale, and good as new!"

A pessimist would say, "I must be the world's unluckiest person! I go out for a simple ordinary walk, because my know-it-all doctor told my wife I need to get more exercise. I check the forecast. Variable clouds, it says. It's sunny and warm when I leave the house. There's no thunder. The clouds aren't even dark. The next thing I know, I'm in the hospital. I'm out of my mind on morphine, and when it wears off, it feels like the bottoms of my feet have been charbroiled and I've got a compound fracture in one leg. The hospital food stinks. I miss a month of work, stuck in bed with nothing to do except read. What did I do to deserve this? What a world, what a world!"

Which would you say?

Optimism means interpreting neutral or ambiguous events in a generally positive way. Of course, it also means expecting good things to happen, to both yourself and others, in both the near and distant future.

In the same way, pessimism means interpreting neutral or ambiguous events, including the future, in a generally negative way. Think of the more outstanding pessimists you know, and how seldom their frightening predictions come true. Oddly, this does not deter them from making new discouraging assessments and predictions. What will change them? Chances are there is nothing you or anyone else can say that will make a difference. However, it is within the pessimist's power to rec-ognize herself as a pessimist and to begin cultivating optimism.

Advantages of Optimism

Optimism versus pessimism is a favorite topic for armchair philosophers. It's pointless to speculate about whether the opti-mists or the pessimists are really correct. The more interesting question is whether the optimists or pessimists are better off. About this, there is no doubt. Pessimism is bad for your mental and physical health, your social life, your marriage, your career, and your overall enjoyment of life. Ask the scientists who have carefully and repeatedly studied the matter.

Of course, an optimistic attitude does not guarantee a long, happy, and successful life. Optimists die in plane crashes about as often as pessimists, and pessimists win the lottery about as often as optimists.

Optimism has its limits. Most dreams don't come true. No one avoids loss, disappointment, and humiliation. However, because optimists do not exaggerate disappointments and because they hope for better days even in the face of misfortune, they take their disappointments more easily.

Pessimists often claim that they are better off than optimists because they are prepared for the worst. This is a logical argument, but there is no good way to prepare for most misfortunes. You deal with them as they occur.

Cultivating Optimism with Compassion

This old story has been told countless times in various forms in many languages.

A traveler leaves North City, headed for Southtown. The towns are about a day's journey apart. The traveler stops halfway along for rest and lunch. He says to the proprietor of the inn, "I'm headed for Southtown. What's it like there?"

The proprietor asks, "Any chance you're coming from North City?"

"Why yes, I just left there this morning."

"How did you find North City?"

The traveler replies, "It was a fine place. The people are not very outgoing, but once you get to know them a little, they're all smiles and generosity. They are the funniest people I ever met. They could make a rock laugh. They're honest, hardworking, churchgoing people, with no airs or pretensions. The homes and gardens are simple, honest, and clean. I was very happy during my visit there."

The innkeeper says, "You'll like Southtown too."

A while later, after the first traveler has left, a second traveler arrives. He says, "I've just come from North City and I'm on my way to Southtown. You know what Southtown is like?"

The innkeeper asks how North City was.

The new traveler replies, "You're joking, right? Everybody must know it's a cruel joke, a nowhere, a traveler's nightmare. The people there wouldn't piss on you if you were on fire. They have their upright churchy ways, but they're totally hypocritical. Half the time you can't figure out what they're talking about and then they bust out laughing like they were loony. And my God, you should see their homes and gardens. These people have raised dismalness to an art form. The three days I spent there seemed like three months."

The innkeeper replies, "Southtown won't be any better."

Before reading further, ask yourself what you might tell a celestial innkeeper about your recent visit to Earth.

_____

_____

_____

_____

Perhaps your report to the innkeeper is a little grim. If so, what would you *like* to be able to say to the innkeeper? Don't try to caricature optimism. Avoid sarcasm. Think of another way to summarize your experiences on Earth that might leave a better taste in your mouth.

_____

_____

_____

_____

These stories are not just about optimism. They are also about Compassion. When viewed from the point of view of your own desires, tastes, and interests, other people may seem dreary and unpleasant. When viewed in the context of their own lives, they become interesting; their feelings and behavior make sense.

If most of the people you meet seem dreary and unpleasant, your whole world will seem dreary and unpleasant. And you may seem particularly dreary and unpleasant to others. Whether you perceive other people as good or bad company, attractive or ugly, interesting or dull depends largely upon your habits of thought.

Temperament no doubt plays a role, too. Some people are much more agreeable than others; some people are much more sociable than others. But you have little or no direct control over your temperament. You have a great deal of control over your habits of thought. If you persistently cultivate compassionate habits of thought despite a disagreeable temperament your temperament might change permanently, as an indirect result.

Learn to view others not as a critic-at-large. Learn to view others as natural phenomena, as you would observe birds, clouds, or flowers. One does not automatically classify birds, clouds, or flowers as good or bad, dull or interesting, and so forth. We presume that each species of bird or flower is here for a reason, and each cloud has its rightful place. We can cultivate the same habits of thought about other people.

When Hindus take their vows of monkhood, they pray, "Let my mind be a bee that seeks the nectar in each person." Yet how often do our minds work like flies that seek out the filth in each person? Either way is equally easy.

If you want to be disappointed in just about every person you meet, here's a simple trick. Look for intelligence in the attractive people you meet. Look for beauty in the successful people you meet. Look for success in the intelligent people you meet. If you meet someone who seems attractive, intelligent, and successful, look for charm or wisdom. With little difficulty, you'll manage to dislike or disapprove of just about everyone you encounter.

The trick can be turned around. In the left-hand column of the chart on the next page, make a quick list of some people you know whom you expect to see in the next few days. In the middle column, think of one unpleasant feature this person has that you sometimes focus upon to the extent that your enjoyment of that person is diminished. In the right-hand column, record one admirable or pleasant feature that you want to remember to focus upon next time you see him or her.

After you have had a chance to see many of these people, make a note of how this procedure might have altered your experience of them. Also record how your experience of people in general might have changed.

Person	Unpleasant feature	Pleasant feature

A previewer named Gerald made these notes:

Person	Unpleasant feature	Pleasant feature
Susan	Boring	Friendly
Fred	Bad taste	Well read
Althea	Too talkative	Funny
Charles	Dull, dull, dull	Kind and patient
Roger	Dresses badly	Supportive
Clarice	Constantly complains	Sensible
Emily	Always in a hurry	Likes me
Dominique	Gets her current events from *People* magazine	Empathic

Gerald wrote:

I didn't expect much from this exercise. It seems pretty obvious. I didn't expect to find that I judge others so harshly. I know I don't always focus on the bad things about these people, but I do it a lot more than I need to. It was nice to have an alternative. I couldn't always remember the good things I planned to look for in the people around me, but that didn't matter too much. The principle was more important. If I couldn't think of the one I had planned on, I found another one, on the spot. This week has seemed nicer than most. I'm looking forward to the rest of my life a little more than usual.

Cultivating Optimism with Attention

Means and ends are two different orientations toward life in general. Some people seem to focus on their goals, others focus on the means they use to reach their goals. If life is a race, we may run for the love of the race, and run at a comfortable pace. Or we may run to win, however much it hurts. Compassion, Attention, and Gratitude emphasize means over ends.

Life is uncertain, and death is certain. Therefore, running to win seems unwise. Running to win will generate pessimism, because nobody wins every race. As age increases and health declines, you'll win fewer and fewer races. When viewed this way, none of us have much to look forward to.

It's odd that professional athletes are said to "play" a sport. Their "play" is deadly serious. As a matter of fact, most professional athletes lose all interest in playing their sport for pleasure. They play to win or don't play at all. Yet "play" comes from an Old English word that means "to leap for joy, dance, or rejoice."

Mihaly Csikszentmihalyi, in his book *Flow: The Psychology of Optimal Experience*, reminds us that people are happiest and most creative and productive when working or playing in a lighthearted way, not because they are determined to succeed, but because they enjoy the activity itself. They might also wish to succeed, but they love the activity whether they succeed or not and may redefine success to fit their capabilities.

According to my habits of thought, I might think of myself as grimly grinding out the work I must perform each day to eat, avoid homelessness, and get health insurance. These are pessimistic habits of thought that will cause me to regard the future with dread.

Other habits of thought will paint a different emotional picture. I might think of myself as working cheerfully at the occupation I have chosen for myself, being a parent to the children I love, pursuing my interests and developing my talents, and so on. Work is still required, of course, and I will still sometimes get tired. Yet looking at exactly the same life in this way is far more optimistic.

Keep in mind that fatigue is not necessarily unpleasant. Fatigue after a long hike or swim or a good game of tennis or chess might be rather pleasurable. Even fatigue after digging a ditch might be pleasurable, depending on the reasons you dug the ditch and your attitude about the task. Fatigue after doing something you resented will seem very unpleasant indeed.

Bring these concerns into your own life, in a personal and specific way, by doing the following exercise. List some of the usual tasks and responsibilities you often perform in the course of a typical workday. If they seem like burdensome tasks that must be done, note how that is so under "Burden." Then reconsider how you might think of them differently so that they might be more pleasurable. You might want to consider how your approach to the activity might need to change so it could become more pleasurable. Algeo's responses (on the next page) might help you get started.

Smile and Breathe

Thich Nhat Hanh, a widely admired Vietnamese Buddhist monk and teacher, particularly emphasizes the following technique. It's simple, and to the casual observer it might even

Activity	Burden	Pleasure

Activity	Burden	Pleasure
Driving to work on the freeway	Ugh! Commuting. What a pain. What a senseless waste of my time.	I'm sitting in a comfortable, pleasant car, listening to music I like and wouldn't otherwise have time to listen to. This is okay!
Grocery shopping	Same routine, week in, week out.	Most people in the world would give anything to shop in a store like this. So, I like it.
Mowing the lawn	I can hardly wait to start doing something important.	Since I have to do it anyway, I'll try mowing the lawn as if it is important.
Balancing the checkbook	Tedium plus anxiety—what a great combination!	I'll take this pile of canceled checks one item at a time. I'll do it fast, do it right, and be glad I did. That is within my power.

seem inconsequential. But it does require mental effort, as does any method of self-improvement or spiritual inquiry. The mental effort produces the results.

For a moment, take time out from your current activity. Pay full attention to your breathing sensations. Ideally, the belly pushes out a little when the breath goes in, and pulls in a little when the breath goes out. Ideally, the chest and shoulders are nearly motionless.

(If the chest and shoulders are doing most of the work, you are probably anxious, whether you realize it or not. That's useful information. Continue the procedure, keeping this understanding in mind. It might help you be less anxious.)

As you inhale and your belly rises, notice the sensation of the cooler air moving over your upper lip, through your nose and head, down your windpipe, and into your lungs. As you exhale and your belly falls, notice the sensation of the warmer air moving out of your lungs, into your windpipe, through your head and nose, and over your upper lip.

Don't make any special effort to alter your breathing rhythm. If you can slow your breathing tempo slightly, in a way that feels natural and comfortable, go ahead.

With a little practice, you can learn to notice your breathing sensations completely and very quickly. If you are tense or in a hurry, it's a little harder, but still not difficult, and it's even more worth doing then.

Once you feel your breathing sensations are in focus, count three consecutive breaths, paying full attention to your breath sensations. Each time you exhale, smile. Smile in a way that feels natural and honest. It's okay if smiling takes a little effort. If only a small smile or a purely interior smile feels natural and honest, then smile that way.

Each time you smile, think, *I smile because I am alive.*

Alternate thoughts to pair with smiling include:

I smile in compassion for all living things.

I smile to celebrate the here-and-now.

I smile a friendly greeting to the universe.

One easily forgets to use this method, even if it usually brings peace and good cheer. Knowing it but not using it confers no benefit. One way to remember to use it is to make appointments with yourself. In the following table, make some notes about situations in which you'd like to try it. Later on, make a record of the results.

Procedures like this express the principle of Attention. When attending to your breath, you plant yourself firmly in the present time and place. When smiling, you suspend value

When and where?	Results

judgments. You emphasize your suspension of value judgments with your affirmations of love and good cheer. In just a few moments, and with just a little effort, you can transform tired, cheerless trudging into running for the love of the race.

Cultivating Optimism with Gratitude

North City and Southtown might just as easily refer to the present and the future as they do to locations and people. If the present feels unfair, harsh, disappointing, and dreary to you, chances are the future will look about the same. That's pessimism. If you skillfully and diligently cultivate Gratitude about the present, the future will likely look more promising. That's optimism.

One way to cultivate optimism is to express overt Gratitude for current circumstances in both word and deed. You can thank the people around you for the cooperative, pleasant things they do for you, even if you consider them imperfect human beings. You can also work expressions of Gratitude for the way things are in your life into routine conversation. Here are some possible examples:

- To your secretary: Doris, I probably don't thank you often enough for being so reliable and honest. You're always here when we need you. We know we can trust you implicitly. So, I'll say it now, "Thank you."

- To your neighbor: Fred, I was just thinking about how we've lived next door to each other for ten years. During that time, you've never hesitated to loan a tool or lend a hand. You keep an eye on the neighborhood to make sure it's safe for our children. You keep your yard looking nice and that's good for the whole neighborhood. I'm lucky to have a neighbor like you, Fred.

- On April 15, to an acquaintance: When I was putting my tax return in the mailbox, I was thinking that democracy may be expensive and inefficient at times, and injustices do occur, but I'm still awfully glad for the opportunity to support a free and democratic government.

- At the roller rink, to another parent: Isn't it lucky that we can take our kids here for happy and safe fun and exercise! Who cares if the place is tacky and the music is too loud.

- At the grocery store, to the clerk: I was having fun pretending I am an immigrant, just arriving from someplace like Bosnia. It was fun to be amazed by all the different stuff I can get for a fairly small sum of money. Sometimes I forget how rich I really am.

Perhaps statements like these sound ridiculous to you. Socially speaking, they are a bit unusual, but if delivered in a natural way and at a suitable time they will not likely appear ridiculous to others. If it feels unnatural to say these things and others like them, it is probably because you are unaccustomed to open expressions of Gratitude.

Make a note of some of the people to whom you might express Gratitude. Prepare for the encounter now, when you have time to reflect, by considering what form your Gratitude might take and which words you might like to use.

Also make a note of some grateful comments you might like to work into your routine conversations in the next few days.

With a little diligence and ingenuity, your present will start to seem more precious and your future more appealing.

Person	What I plan to say

When, where, or who	What I plan to say

14

C, A, and G in
the Workplace

Consider this recent scientific experiment involving job satisfaction.

A team of doctors obtained MRI images of the lower backs of all employees for a large company. The doctors rated the MRI images for objective evidence of spine disease, with no other knowledge of the workers. At the same time, each worker took a job-satisfaction questionnaire. Several years later, the scientists went back to the same company to find out which workers suffered lower-back pain. There was no relationship between lower-back pain and the spinal MRI images. On the other hand, the job-satisfaction questionnaire strongly predicted who would develop lower-back pain.

Were the workers with sore backs just faking? Probably not. If you dislike your job, or simply endure your job, chances are you will hate your whole life. In turn, your body will punish you. Aches and pains that might seem trivial under other circumstances will seem enormous. You will often feel tired. Insults, frustrations, and disappointments that might seem trivial under other circumstances will take on monstrous proportions. Your whole life might seem like a series of unfair punishments.

Do I exaggerate? Read the Dilbert comic strip with these statements in mind. Dilbert hates his job. His whole life seems to be a series of unfair punishments. He can't get a date, and even his dog doesn't respect him.

Letting Your Work Be Sacred

Imagine Dilbert's insensitive, incompetent boss telling him that his work should be sacred to him. It's a grotesque fantasy, which might actually end up in the comics someday. Of course, the Dilbert comic strip is grotesquely pessimistic. That's why it's funny. If it reflects the true state of the American economy and the true condition of the American worker, we are in big trouble. Keep in mind that the comic strip reflects the way a particular person might caricature the insensitivity and incompetence he sees at his workplace. Another employee at the same workplace, even with the same boss, might see things quite differently.

In any workplace, if you expect to find insensitivity and incompetence you will find it. If you expect to find *only* insensitivity and incompetence you will find little else. Although Dilbert seems like a pleasant and intelligent guy, he expects to find little else but insensitivity and incompetence. His expectations are self-fulfilling. He does teach at least one valuable lesson, though. Whether or not you consider your work sacred is nobody's business but your own. If your boss makes it her business, you are both in trouble. Considering your work sacred is an opportunity that you must fit to your situation and personality. It is certainly not a duty.

If you honestly considered your job sacred, what would that mean and how would you approach it?

I'm not using the word in the religious sense, of course. I use it here to mean something like "regarded with reverence." When your work is sacred it is not just a source of income or a stepping-stone to better things. Instead, you perceive your work as something inherently valuable and worthy of respect or reverence. You feel intuitively that performing your job makes a small but important and lasting difference in the world, a difference you can feel proud of even if it is never widely acknowledged. Every job is potentially sacred and every job is also potentially banal or profane.

C. S. Lewis, the Christian author, wrote, "A man who is eating or lying with his wife or preparing to go to sleep in humility, thankfulness, and temperance, is, by Christian standards, in an infinitely higher state than one who is listening to Bach or reading Plato in a state of pride."

Lewis can be paraphrased in more secular terms with regard to the workplace: The man who is working an unremarkable job in humility, thankfulness, and temperance is in an infinitely more blessed state than one who is running a multinational corporation in a state of arrogance and greed.

Where does one apply for sacred jobs, and how well do they pay? The bad news is the same as the good news. Respect, awe, and reverence are not things that the job gives to the worker. If they happen at all, the worker brings them to the job. The worker brings them to the job by developing habits of thought that support respect, awe, and reverence for his or her work.

How would you behave, speak, and feel differently if you could learn to consider your work sacred? The question leaves room for debate, but these items represent some basic possibilities:

- You might not complain much about the job, nor would you often consider it demeaning or tedious.

- You might not feel ashamed or embarrassed about your job.

- You would often remind yourself that you are doing something that matters, regardless of what other people think.

- You might try to perform one task at a time so you could give each task your full attention.

- You might take pride in doing your job skillfully and correctly, even if that sometimes took extra time or effort.

- You might make an effort to treat coworkers with respect and kindness, whether or not they seemed to have earned it. After all, if your work is sacred, theirs must be sacred, too.

- At the end of a workday or when a task was completed, you might look back and say, "I'm glad I had the opportunity to do that. I'm glad I did it as well as I was able."

If any other possibilities occur to you, record them here:

_____

_____

_____

_____

_____

Respond to each of these items as honestly as you can:

Letting My Work Be Sacred

1. I do one task at a time, giving it my full attention.

    Almost always   Usually   Sometimes   Rarely   Hardly ever

2. When I must talk with someone about my job, I give that person my full attention.

    Almost always   Usually   Sometimes   Rarely   Hardly ever

3. I disparage or ridicule my work.

    Hardly ever   Rarely   Sometimes   Usually   Almost always

4. I consider other jobs to be more important than my job.

    Hardly ever   Rarely   Sometimes   Usually   Almost always

5. I am embarrassed about the work I do.

    Hardly ever   Rarely   Sometimes   Usually   Almost always

6. I see my work only as a way of getting a paycheck.

    Hardly ever   Rarely   Sometimes   Usually   Almost always

7. Positions I hope to hold in the future seem much more important than the position I hold now.

    Hardly ever   Rarely   Sometimes   Usually   Almost always

8. I resent how my work uses up time and energy I would rather spend doing other things.

    Hardly ever   Rarely   Sometimes   Usually   Almost always

9. When I complete a workday, I review it in my mind, thinking, *I did my job as well as I could, and I'm proud of what I accomplished.*

    Almost always   Usually   Sometimes   Rarely   Hardly ever

10. If I had to continue doing the same job I do now for a long time, I would be filled with regret.

    Completely untrue   Mostly untrue   Neutral   Partly true   Certainly true

11. I feel that time spent working on my job is somehow wasted or stolen from me.

| Hardly ever | Rarely | Sometimes | Usually | Almost always |

This questionnaire is arranged so that greater reverence is at the left end of each response and less reverence is at the right end of each response.

Go back over each response with a differently colored pencil or pen and circle the response immediately to the left of your actual response (unless your original response was at the far left). Spend a few minutes reflecting on how your work life (and also, perhaps, your personal life) would be different if you had answered the second way instead of the first. In particular, ask yourself the following questions:

- Would the quality of my life improve?

- Would the quality of my work improve?

- Would my relationships with coworkers improve?

- Would my self-esteem improve?

- Is there any way I would be worse off than I am now?

Compassion on the Job

Human problems are the biggest source of job dissatisfaction. Managers complain of stupidity, incompetence, and bad manners among workers. Workers complain of the same problems among managers. Workers often find other workers lazy, foolish, abrasive, dishonest, hypocritical, tyrannical, disorganized, incompetent, alcoholic, crazy, or otherwise difficult.

For the sake of clarity and brevity, in the rest of this discussion I'll refer to all these difficulties with other people, and others like them, as "inconvenient flaws in others."

Concern for inconvenient flaws in others is not confined to the workplace, of course. This is the biggest single source of aggravation in daily life *outside* of the workplace as well. Yet, somehow, people seem to get more upset about flaws in others at work than at home or in other settings. Perhaps that is because people who inconvenience us with their personal flaws away from work tend to be our relatives and friends. Humans generally tend to cut more slack for relatives and friends.

I don't deny the significance of inconvenient personal flaws in human affairs. There are plenty of misguided people out there doing various forms of harm. Nevertheless, it's usually pointless to be angry about someone else's flaws. The people in question probably don't get it, and might not even know how you feel. Your anger mostly harms yourself.

It's also worth considering that, in the big picture, smart, competent, and hardworking people probably do more harm than lazy and incompetent people. A few thousand innocent people are injured each year because stupid lazy drivers don't bother to use their turn signals. Many times that number are maimed or killed by abandoned land mines each year. These were invented, manufactured, and ordered into place by smart hardworking people. Smart people with good intentions invented Freon and then pumped it into the atmosphere in huge quantities. Perhaps they had blind spots. But all humans, present company included, have blind spots.

When you encounter inconvenient flaws in your coworkers, try one of the following affirmations, modified as necessary to fit the person and situation. All humans are fallible. These aphorisms, derived from the principle of Compassion, affirm the basic humanity of others who present inconvenient flaws. Normally, affirmations are used to cultivate confidence and respect for yourself, but they can just as easily be used to cultivate Compassion for others, and for many other purposes.

- This person didn't ask to be stupid. It just happened, like being tall or short.

- God equally loves dull and clever people.

- Being unkind to this person won't improve his cooperativeness.

- It's not within my power to improve this person's social skills.

- If this person were as capable and vigorous as I am, I wouldn't be her boss.

- Incompetence in this particular job does not make this person worthless.

- I am not paid to judge people. I am paid to do my job as well as I can, with the understanding that others will sometimes get in the way.

- But for fortune, *I* could be poorly educated and *he* could have the degree.

- Maybe I am more honest than this person. That isn't *my* misfortune; it's hers. Even if she is winning this particular battle through dishonesty, she will eventually pay a terrible price.

In the left-hand column of the table below, try making an inventory of coworkers who frequently inconvenience you with their personal flaws. Find an affirmation from the foregoing list suitable for that particular inconvenient person, modify it as needed, and record it in the middle column. This will help you remember what frame of mind you want to be in the next time you have a challenging encounter with this particular person. After the encounter, if you remembered to use the affirmation you planned, you might like to record the outcome in the right-hand column.

Name of inconvenient person	Affirmation	Results

Attention on the Job

Whenever I see bumper stickers that say, "I'd Rather Be Fishing," or something of this nature, I feel sorry for the person displaying it. Sometimes during my lunch break, I take a slow drive along the river. There I see quite a few people who are fishing because they don't have anything else to do, and no money to do anything else with. They'd rather be working.

Of course, it is not really evil to think that you'd rather be somewhere else. Nevertheless, in most cases, it's foolish and self-destructive. Jon Kabat-Zinn called his popular book on mindfulness *Wherever You Go, There You Are.* The title largely tells the tale: If you are fishing, fish. Do it as well as you can, and enjoy it as much as possible. If you are working, work. Do it as well as you can and enjoy *that* as much as possible. If you can't enjoy your work, don't deliberately make it worse than it is by nursing resentment and disappointment about it. This is why I have a license-plate frame that says, "I'd Rather Be Right Here, Right Now."

Right now, I'm in my office, at my keyboard, writing this chapter on a day most people consider a holiday. My wife and children are at home. I enjoy being at home on a holiday with my wife and children. Here at the office all alone, a little restless and frustrated, things are not too jolly. Still, I am free to choose different ways of thinking about my situation.

If I choose, I can think, *I wish I didn't have to do this today. I wish I were home playing with the kids and reading my new book.* Alternately, I can think, *I've wanted to finish this manuscript for a long time, and I'm happy to have the opportunity to publish it. Today is a good day to get some work done.* I might add, *If I were at home taking it easy, I would feel bad about not working on this.*

If I am in the habit of thinking, *I wish I didn't have to do this today,* chances are I will feel depressed, tired, or resentful while working. I won't have a good day, and I won't get much done, which means, of course, that I'll have to spend other days doing the same thing. I could get into a pretty deep rut that way.

If you are often angry, dissatisfied, or restless about your job, consider the ways your habitual thoughts make your job seem worse than it has to be. Chances are, these habitual thoughts and beliefs express unnecessary value judgments or focus on the past or future instead of the present.

Some previewers volunteered to identify habitual thoughts and beliefs about their jobs that contradict the principle of Attention. They then formulated alternate thoughts. On the next page are some of their responses.

Try the same exercise for yourself. You may not be able to identify nonattentive habits of thought about your work right away. You might want to carry a notebook with you at work so you can record them as you recognize them. Later on, you can dispute them and consider alternate habits of thought.

Habitual attentive thoughts and beliefs about job	Alternative nonattentive thoughts and beliefs about job
I didn't go to college so I could run a cash register.	I'm here, I'm doing what I need to do right now, so what's the problem?
I'm so bored, I'll go nuts at any moment!	I can concentrate on my work or I can concentrate on how bored I am. I think I'll concentrate on my work.
I wish I could work with my brains instead of my back.	Next time a better job comes along I'll take it. In the meantime, this beats the heck out of unemployment.
I'm an engineer, but I have to spend my days listening to lame excuses, lies, and perpetual whining from my subordinates instead of accomplishing something useful.	Only an engineer could supervise my subordinates. It's a job that must be done, and it might as well be me.

Habitual thoughts and beliefs about my job	Alternative thoughts and beliefs about my job

Below, record how your feelings about your job change as you do this exercise.

_____

_____

_____

_____

_____

Robert wrote:

I've always taken it for granted that a job is a thing to be resented. It never occurred to me that I might have some chance of being comfortable in a job. I've been especially resentful in my present job, which pays poorly and doesn't give me any respect. It never occurred to me that I am free to treat it as if it is worth doing and at least theoretically worthy of admiration. This makes all the difference.

Gratitude on the Job

Every job provides many reasons for resentment and many other reasons for Gratitude. Resentment comes naturally, Gratitude doesn't. Accordingly, many people resent their jobs. One rarely hears deeply felt expressions of Gratitude about a job. But workers are free to choose either Gratitude or resentment; both represent habits of thought.

Why choose Gratitude? Gratitude feels good. Grateful people are more popular, more eager and enthusiastic, perhaps more creative. Why reject resentment? Resentment feels bad. Resentful people are less likable. Resentment drains energy, enthusiasm, and creativity.

Gratitude suggests subtle but deeply felt pleasure, often for small ordinary things. But it has an additional connotation that is hard to pin down: feeling pleasure about something that you *don't take for granted*. Taking life's pleasures—small or large—for granted makes all the difference.

For example, if you've been unwillingly unemployed for a long time and then you get a new job that pays better than you had dared hope for, you might secretly kiss your first paycheck and feel it glowing warmly all afternoon in your pocket until you put it in the bank. That's because you don't take that one for granted. A year later, your paycheck might be even bigger, but chances are by then you feel entitled to it, you tend to spend it before you receive it, and you wish it were bigger. The impulse to kiss it is all gone, along with the warm glow in your pocket.

Gratitude is a special kind of pleasure, though not necessarily an intense pleasure. It is a subtle, secret pleasure you feel in your bones and deep down in your belly. Gratitude is the single thing that makes life most worth living.

Each job provides somewhat different opportunities for both Gratitude and resentment. No job is perfectly good. Few jobs are perfectly bad. Use the following chart to reflect upon the various ways that you might experience genuine Gratitude for your job more often or more deeply.

In the left-hand column you'll find a series of possibilities for Gratitude about your work. No one will endorse all of these possibilities. Which ones you endorse will depend partly on your circumstances and partly on your particular temperament. In the center column, indicate how often you actually experience Gratitude about that particular item. In the right-hand column, mark an X to indicate each item for which you want to cultivate greater Gratitude.

Possible area for Gratitude	Never Rarely Sometimes Often	Emphasize new Gratitude
1. Able to make my living by producing a worthy product or service.		
2. Participate in a company that provides good jobs to many workers.		
3. Grateful to be employed at all.		
4. Interesting work.		
5. Pleasant working conditions.		
6. Good salary and benefits.		
7. Opportunity to serve customers.		
8. Friendship with coworkers.		
9. Coworkers who really look out for me.		

10. Able to do the kind of work I can take pride in.		
11. Work for a boss who really tries to be fair.		
12. Work for a boss who is truly competent.		
13. Work for a boss who takes good care of her subordinates.		
14. Subordinates who really do their best.		
15. Subordinates who appreciate my skill.		

Before leaving this exercise behind, reconsider some of the items you might have considered utterly incompatible with Gratitude. For example, if you really dislike your boss, you may have responded *No way* to all boss-related items. However, is it possible that your boss really tries to be fair even though he is incompetent? Or perhaps he really does take care of his subordinates, on the whole, even though he is somewhat capricious?

In the same way, you may feel the product or service you help produce is too banal to feel grateful about. Consequently, you may have automatically ruled out Gratitude for the opportunity to produce a worthy product. Take laundry detergent, for example. It is not exciting. Nonetheless, laundry detergent is a useful product and the world is a slightly better place because high quality, inexpensive laundry detergent is available in abundance. Although it may seem absurd at first, there is a tiny possibility that you could feel grateful about that item after all. Reconsider the other items in a similar manner.

15

C, A, and G in

Family Life

Ever heard the saying that a woman needs a man like a fish needs a bicycle? Or what about this joke: God came to Adam early in his residence in the Garden of Eden and asked him if there was anything he wanted. Adam replied, "I'm lonely. I'd like to have a companion. Someone who will always be fascinating and companionable, a joy to be with ... you get the idea?"

God replies, "I can do it, but it'll cost you an arm and a leg!"

Adam asks, "What can I get for a rib?"

Children are not excluded from this continuing humor battle. A popular bumper sticker reads, "Insanity is hereditary. You get it from your kids."

All joking is half true. Thousands of jokes and witticisms like this reflect widespread unhappiness in family life. More than half of all marriages undertaken this year will end in divorce. Three quarters of unmarried couples who begin living together this year will eventually separate, permanently. By then, many will have bought homes, conceived children, and planned lives together. No more than one American child in five grows up in a household in which their parents are consistently kind, affectionate, and loyal to each other, and remain married throughout their lives.

I don't think it's an exaggeration to say that divorce is the number-one public health problem in America. This is equally true of other industrialized countries around the world. Divorce leads to poor health, depression, bankruptcy, drug and alcohol abuse, crime, and even suicide. As a rule, children from divorced families grow up to be less happy and less successful than others. Insensitive, thoughtless parenting is probably the second greatest public health problem in America. Consider the prison population, for instance. It has become a nation within the borders of our nation. In many states, we now spend more on prisons than we do on education. Very few of these unfortunate (and often dangerous) men and women grew up in loving, stable homes.

Yet most divorces can be prevented and most married couples honestly wish to stay married. Most parents want to be the best parents they can be. The couples who seek out my services for marital counseling usually have fixable problems. Those that don't could have fixed their problems if they had tried sooner. The same goes for family problems involving children and teenagers as well as stepfamily problems.

These things are both sad and encouraging. They're sad because so many preventable misfortunes occur in family life. They're encouraging because it's nice to know that most families can do better—much better.

It's possible to buy books full of excellent advice on how to solve marriage and family problems. Other books, equally successful, seem silly or potentially harmful. What's a book consumer to do? Anchor your efforts to the principles of Compassion, Attention, and Gratitude. If these principles have made sense to you in other settings and provided good results, there is a good chance you will be equally satisfied by their impact on the quality of your marriage and family life.

Compassion in Marriage and Family Life

I know a man who berates his wife every day of his life, at about the same time each day for about the same reasons. He thinks he has good reason to berate his wife. She is a terrible housekeeper, a terrible cook, and she spends a great deal of time in bed feeling ill, though innumerable doctors have failed to find anything wrong with her. One day I asked this man if he thinks his wife is doing the best she can. He was startled by my question. "What's that got to do with it?" he asked. I asked him if she had ever promised to be an excellent cook or housekeeper. This startled him too. "Why are you defending her?" he wanted to know.

The best spouses disappoint us occasionally. In average marriages, spouses often disappoint each other. I know a number of very pleasant and responsible adults who tell me they have always been a disappointment to their parents. Nature has played a practical joke on the human race. Children usually don't excel at the things their parents value most. Spouses often turn out not to be the people you thought they were when you fell in love with them.

If you are a spouse who often feels disappointed, Compassion can help. If you are a spouse who often disappoints, Compassion can help. The same goes for parents who are disappointed with their children and vice versa.

In the left column list the most important ways your spouse or child disappoints you.

Disappointment	Doing best?	More anger or criticism?

For each item, reflect for a moment on whether your spouse or child is doing the best she can do in this area, given her talents, personality, circumstances, and so on. Record your answer in the center column. How do you know if she's doing the best she can? You can't know for sure, but you probably know her better than anyone else, so you can probably guess correctly. Recall the things you've said to each other about it. Recall the things the two of you have done to try to solve the problem. Ask your intuition. Ask your mother.

Now reflect on whether more criticism and anger from you will improve the situation. Consider how many times you have already criticized or blamed on this topic, and what results you have produced.

In many cases, it is clear that, for the time being, the disappointing spouse (or child) is doing the best she can do, and that more criticism and blaming will not improve the situation. That's often easy to see. The tougher question is what to do next.

In family life, just as in the rest of life, you have three basic choices when confronting a problem.

- Find the ingenuity and determination needed to change it.

- Cultivate serenity about it, because it can't be changed in the foreseeable future.

- Slowly go nuts complaining about it while trying to fix it, even when you know it won't do any good.

Many modern, educated Americans are appalled by the suggestion that they might have to settle for something less than a perfectly satisfying marriage or a perfect child. They have grown up with the misguided idea that they are entitled to get what they want, and that they are particularly entitled to a satisfactory spouse or flawless child. If a spouse or child disappoints, they think there is a problem that must be fixed immediately.

Scientific research on marital and family happiness easily proves this view is wrong. Flawed partners or children don't harm families. Repeated bitter disputes harm families. Of all the questions you might ask a couple about their marriage, there is only one that clearly indicates overall marital satisfaction and predicts the likelihood of divorce. That question is, "How often do you and your spouse have bitter, painful conflict?" If the answer is "pretty often" or "very often," that couple's odds are poor, and they are not likely enjoying their marriage. If the answer is "seldom" or "rarely," that couple has a good chance of a long and happy marriage terminated by old age and death, not divorce.

Of course, people do change, but when they do it's rarely to avoid the disapproval of others. Sometimes people change in order to please themselves. Sometimes they do it because they honestly hope to please someone else. Instead of focusing on how your mate disappoints you, you might consider the likelihood that you are equally disappointing to your mate. Are you interested in changing to please your mate? Record some of the ways you might try to become a better mate or parent to please *yourself.*

One important expression of Compassion is treating someone else with kindness and generosity even when he has disappointed you. As with other forms of Compassion, there is no guarantee that the other person will appreciate you for it or respond in kind. Remember, that isn't the reason you do it. You practice Compassion because it is inherently worthwhile, and as a secondary benefit you'll find that doing so brings out the best in others.

Disciplined Compassion

Some misguided parents, in the name of Compassion, refuse to enforce or even make rules for their children. Some misguided spouses, in the name of Compassion, don't let their partners know their expectations. This is unfortunate, and it gives Compassion a bad name. If we hope that Compassion will catch on in this world, we must demonstrate that compassionate people can be tough and practical when necessary.

Married partners need to understand each other very clearly on certain topics. Married partners need to communicate to each other what behavior they will not tolerate. Although married partners might be deeply committed to each other and deeply in love with each other, each must understand that the other will refuse to tolerate certain forms of misbehavior.

With a couple of adjustments, these guidelines apply equally well to relations between parents and teenagers. Of course, with children the playing field is not entirely level. The parents will make most of the rules and dispense most of the consequences. Still, there is nothing wrong with a teenager clarifying his expectations of his parents and requiring some kind of compensation if they break their promises.

I encourage couples to sit down and discuss the following possibilities, and others like them. Most couples think it's silly and unnecessary because they love each other. I hope they don't find out the hard way that love does not conquer all.

What would you do if:

- you found out I am having an affair?

- you find out I had an affair in the past?

- you found out I was hiding some of my income from you?

- I beat one of the children?

- I beat you?

- I started drinking heavily and wouldn't stop?

- I refused to do my fair share around the house?

- I frequently stayed out late and wouldn't tell you where I was?

- I often spent money on things we couldn't afford?

Compassion does not always preclude punishment or retaliation, as long as these are done in a compassionate way. This must be so, or civilized life cannot continue. If your home is burglarized, Compassion does not prevent you from calling the police. Compassion *would* prevent you from shooting the burglar in the back as he flees the scene of the crime. If a subordinate is poorly motivated and incompetent, Compassion does not prevent you from firing him. Compassion *does* prevent you from firing him in a way that humiliates and discourages him.

In the same way, Compassion does not prevent you from saying to your spouse, "If you began beating the children, and you weren't sorry and didn't stop doing it, I would take the children and move back to Montana, get a restraining order against you, and thereafter only communicate with you by mail."

In the case of children and teenagers, happy families must have rules. Some rules are more compassionate than others. The most compassionate family rules are clear and consistent and acknowledge that inevitable human emotions apply to all family members, not just the children. Rules like these implicitly recognize the humanity of the children *and* the parents. In general, the most compassionate punishments are just harsh enough to let the children know that the parents are serious about enforcing the rules. Except in cases of extreme misbehavior, compassionate consequences usually expire in twenty-four hours or less. Compassionate discipline of children usually includes just as many rewards for good behavior as punishments for bad. In many cases, compassionate rules will normally seem fair and reasonable to the children involved.

To illustrate, a father I know was having a lot of trouble with his teenage daughter, who he felt had a "smart mouth." The mother felt torn because she felt both her daughter and her husband were behaving badly. In just a few minutes, all parties agreed to the following set of rules about their arguments.

Johnson Family Rules

1. Mom and Dad agree that they will patiently listen to Tammy's requests, comments, and criticisms whenever possible, as long as she is polite and respectful.

2. Tammy agrees that Mom and Dad have the right to refuse to listen, and she understands that they will listen to her whenever possible.

3. Tammy agrees not to argue when Mom and Dad say, "We don't want to discuss this."

4. All parties agree that discussions should end by mutual agreement whenever possible.

5. Tammy agrees that when Mom or Dad say, "The discussion is over," she will end the discussion.

6. Tammy agrees that Mom and Dad are in charge and they have the right to make rules, set standards, say no, and give consequences.

7. Violations of this agreement by Tammy constitute a violation of the "no arguing" rule, and will likely result in some kind of punishment. Tammy is entitled to one warning.

8. Mom and Dad agree to do a special favor for Tammy if they break this agreement.

Tammy and her parents all signed and dated this agreement. To her father's surprise, Tammy loved the agreement. Arguing stopped almost immediately.

Attention in Marriage and Family Life

When I work with marriages and family problems involving teenagers, I invariably find that the feuding parties don't actually listen to each other and, in turn, don't feel heard. What happens instead is that when one party is speaking, the other party is preparing his rebuttal instead of listening. Here's an example:

Husband: Every time I ask you what's for dinner you have this, like, seizure or something. I can't figure it out.

Wife: You think that you're the only one in this family who has a job. I have two jobs!

Husband: I cook. I shop. I don't get it. What's the problem?

Wife: Yeah, precisely. You don't get it. That's the problem.

Husband: So should I try to read your mind or something? Is there a tiny indicator light on your forehead that tells me if it's okay to ask, or what?

Wife: We have a chart that says when we're supposed to cook. We're supposed to plan the meals we're responsible for.

Husband: When my foot is in a cast and you have the week off?

Wife: I had to take this week off, or I'd lose the vacation time. Frankly, I'd rather be at work. If my foot was in a cast, I would be at work.

Therapist to wife: Can you tell me what your husband is trying to say to you?

Wife: He's trying to tell me he expects me to do the cooking when he's not in the mood.

Therapist to husband: Can you tell me what your wife is trying to say to you?

Husband: Yeah. If she's totally rude and uncivilized, it's my fault.

Similar exchanges between a parent and a teenager are easy to imagine.

The problem with pointless and destructive exchanges like this is that neither party is listening to what the other person is actually saying. This violates the principle of Attention. In exchanges like this, each party has a fixed idea of what the other person "should" think and "should" feel. These expectations generate endless complaints from both sides, but no actual exchange of views. Both parties pay more attention to the past and future than the present. As a result, both parties feel, for good reason, that the other is not listening. Both parties fail to recognize that *they* are not listening, either.

Taking the time to ascertain what the other party actually means to say offers an added advantage. It slows down the pace of the discussion. When a discussion about a sensitive topic goes too fast, a rapid series of mutual escalations can appear in just seconds. These normally end in mutual explosions of anger.

The next time you experience a husband-wife or parent-child dispute, try using these simple guidelines derived from the principle of Attention.

- Choose a topic and stay on it. Save the others for later.

- Focus your Attention on what the other person is trying to say to you right now.

- Resist the temptation to evaluate the other person's comments as right or wrong, fair or unfair, and so on. It will take time for both of you to agree on what is correct or fair. Give the discussion the time it needs.

- Focus more on the quality of the exchange and less on the outcome you hope to achieve. In other words, focus more on means and less on ends. If the exchange is courteous and patient and both people participate about equally, the outcome will likely take care of itself.

- Each time the other person concludes a comment, demonstrate that you were really listening by summarizing what you heard the other person say. Do so without editorial comments, particularly sarcastic comments. (In such circumstances, editorial comments are a form of unnecessary value judgment.)

- Follow these guidelines even if your partner doesn't.

If the husband and wife in the previous example had followed these suggestions, the conversation would have gone more like this:

Husband: Every time I ask you what's for dinner you have this, like, seizure or something. I can't figure it out.

Wife: Let me see if I understand this. You think I have a problem with you asking me what's for dinner. Is that right?

Husband: Well, duh! Do I have to hire a skywriter? [A nasty editorial comment. Wisely, the wife lets it pass, unremarked.]

Wife: Okay, I understand. Well, the problem isn't that you ask what's for dinner. The problem is, you ask me when it's your night to cook. That makes me crazy. It seems totally insulting to me, and you've broken your promise, too.

Husband:	Hmmm . . . do you mean to suggest that I'm lying and manipulating?
Wife:	I don't know. You're honest about most things. That's why I can't understand how this thing happens with dinner.
Husband:	Okay, so you think I'm honest about most things, but you feel I am not acting in good faith if I ask you what's for dinner when you think it's my night to cook. Is that right?
Wife:	Yeah, exactly. Why do I have to keep explaining this to you? [Rhetorical questions are almost always editorial comments, better withheld.]
Husband:	How many times have I told you that I don't always know whose turn it is to cook? [Another rhetorical comment.] Life is complicated. You can't just go by a chart!
Wife:	You want me to understand that you don't always know whose turn it is to cook. Right?
Husband:	Right. I know we have this chart, but it is out of date and it doesn't cover every situation that comes up.

In spite of provocations from both sides, the husband and wife start to understand each other better at this point.

Gratitude in Bed

Although it may not be immediately obvious, Compassion, Attention, and Gratitude can be sexy.

The following procedure focuses primarily on Gratitude, although Attention and Compassion will come into play as well. Although this procedure begins with sex, it isn't *just* sex. Mutual appreciation, respect, and enjoyment are just as important whether you're naked alone in bed together or cleaning out the garage together.

Husband and wife should use separate worksheets. In some cases, the level of honesty might be too high with these worksheets. It might be best for partners to keep them private from one another.

A happy marriage is not necessary for a completely satisfactory life, nor does it guarantee a happy life. Only a few marriages will ever approach the modern ideal of enduring romantic passion, sexual lust, endless fun, and unwavering friendship. It's likely that the most satisfying marriages involve two spouses who help each other strive for some mutually desirable and beneficial goal. This may be part of the reason that religious fundamentalists are less likely to divorce than other couples. Whether or not you and your partner are religious fundamentalists, wanting what you have is a mutually desirable and beneficial goal you can spend your lives striving for, sometimes as individuals and sometimes as partners. As your children get older, you can invite them to join you. Along the way, Compassion, Attention, and Gratitude will help you enjoy each other more and be kinder to each other.

Much sexual pleasure is destroyed by unnecessary value judgments about physical appearance, both yours and your partner's. Try having sex while blindfolded—not because it's kinky and supposedly thrilling, but because the blindfold interrupts your usual concern about your own appearance and your partner's appearance. Pay attention to smells, sounds, and tactile sensations instead of appearances. Record your reactions to the experience:

_____

_____

_____

_____

Fantasies are inevitable and can be exciting. They can also be repetitive and boring and cut you off from your partner. Have sex in the usual way, but stay in the present as much as possible, paying full attention to each moment, each gesture, each sensation, as fully as possible. Avoid your usual fantasies. Record your reactions to the experience:

_____

_____

_____

_____

It's easy to focus on disappointments and frustrations about routine lovemaking. However, there is usually much to be grateful for. Try making love in the usual way, but before beginning spend five minutes reflecting on all that there is to be grateful for in the forthcoming experience. Record some of your reflections, either before or after:

_____

_____

_____

_____

While making love in the usual way, slow down the pace a little. From time to time reflect for a moment on what there is to be grateful for in the present sexual experience. Later on, record your reflections:

_____

_____

_____

_____

_____

After making love in the usual way, take a few moments to reflect upon what there was to be grateful for in that particular sexual experience. When you have the chance, record your reflections:

_____

_____

_____

_____

_____

Consider sharing some of the foregoing with your partner, as you see fit. What happens?

_____

_____

_____

_____

_____

If your partner shares some of his/her sexual Gratitude with you, make a record of what he/she said and how you felt about it.

_____

_____

_____

_____

_____

16

Courtship and Romantic Love

According to my unmarried adult clients, the problem of courtship combines the mental challenge of calculus with the anxiety of juggling chain saws and the odds of the state lottery.

Widespread dread about courtship is similar to widespread dread about public speaking, the most common and intense of all phobias. In both cases, the dread is understandable, though unnecessary. In both cases, the problem revolves around the fear of appearing foolish. It *is* somewhat painful to appear foolish when speaking in public or when approaching a possible romantic partner. However, in both cases the risk is exaggerated, and even if one does occasionally appear foolish, the actual harm is small. Awkward, quavering speeches are soon forgotten, as are dull evenings with shy partners.

In any case, anyone who wants to get over the dread of public speaking can certainly succeed. Few speaking-phobics will become talented orators, but oratorical talent is not necessary for making a successful public presentation. In the same way, anyone who wants to get over the dread of courtship can do so. Once again, few people will become another Rudolph Valentino or Marilyn Monroe, but this is not necessary in a satisfactory romantic partner.

Dread of public speaking is mostly a nuisance or, in some occupations, a modest obstacle to success. Persistent loneliness resulting from courtship dread is much sadder, though equally preventable.

Tommy represents a typical example of courtship dread. He's a nice guy, not handsome and not ugly, neither rich nor poor, not bright and not dumb. He lives alone, goes to an okay job every day, visits his nine-year-old son regularly, and feels very lonely for romantic love and sex. He complains, "No one wants to date me. Every time I get interested in a woman, I get shot down." When I ask him, "When was the last time you asked a woman out or asked her for her phone number?" he replies, "It wouldn't do any good, so I've pretty much stopped asking." He thinks it's been a couple of years since he last asked.

Tommy wants to date but doesn't want to get rejected. That's like wanting to hit home runs without ever striking out—it can't be done. Babe Ruth didn't just lead the league in home runs; he also led in strikeouts. Tommy thinks he can't bear rejection, but he hates loneliness. He would be fine if he could learn to strike out cheerfully. Compassion, Attention, and Gratitude can help. (More on this later.)

In addition to fear of rejection, a few other problems arise frequently in courtship.

Alathea, for instance, doesn't mind dating. Occasional rejections don't trouble her much. She just can't find anybody she cares for. She sometimes sleeps with guys for whom she has lukewarm feelings, and then wishes she hadn't. At other times, she continues to date a guy who's crazy about her even though she doesn't consider him a keeper—just because he's a nice guy and she doesn't want to hurt his feelings.

What's Alathea's problem? Maybe guilt prevents her from rejecting partners who aren't suitable. Compassion, Attention, and Gratitude can make that easier for her. Maybe she has trouble making the transition from liking to loving, even when she has a promising partner. Applying the three principles can help her there, too.

Then of course there is the problem of falling in love too fast or too indiscriminately. Men do this more than women. I know a woman, now middle-aged, who tells me that on half a dozen occasions, men have pleaded with her to marry them on the first date, sometimes before they arrived at the restaurant! This is not an exclusively male problem, however. Notorious and dangerous male criminals routinely get offers of marriage from women who know them only from news reports.

The Four Basic Skills

There is a small number of skills necessary for successful courtship. None is hard to understand. None is impossible to obtain.

If you're missing any one of them, you will probably have courtship trouble. The prerequisite skills are:

- *Rejecting with kindness and poise.* On average, you have to kiss about ten frogs to find one prince or princess. You'll have to reject those frogs (though some may reject you first).

- *Getting rejected with poise and good cheer.* You will seem a prince or princess to some new friends. To some others, you will appear distinctly froglike and will be rejected accordingly.

- *Stepping on the gas.* If you have a very promising new partner but feel lukewarm, it might be possible to accelerate your romantic emotions.

- *Stepping on the brake.* You might have strong feelings for a new friend who would probably make a horrible life partner. Or you might simply be falling in love faster than your new friend, causing discomfort for both of you.

Throughout this chapter, I'll concentrate on how Compassion, Attention, and Gratitude can facilitate all four of these basic skills.

Rejecting with Compassion

It's hard to reject a nice, normal person who doesn't happen to light your fire. You might wonder if your standards are too high. If you can't explain your lack of interest, you might feel foolish. Your partner may feel hurt or angry; he might challenge you. "What are you looking for that I don't have?" he might ask. Under such circumstances, it's tempting to try to think of a good reason. Yet often there is no good reason. Scientists don't understand why one possible partner appeals and another, apparently similar, doesn't appeal at all. The same phenomenon occurs in wolves and other animals that generally bond in pairs.

Inventing a good reason or exaggerating an unimportant one is a face-saving maneuver, or it might be an honest attempt at kindness. Still, if you have no clear reason, it's better to be honest about it. Even if you think you have a definite reason, it might be wise to doubt it or withhold it. You might think, for instance, *I could never love someone with a gap between his front teeth. That look has never appealed to me.* This kind of reason is hardly convincing. It's more likely a face-saving maneuver. Don't bet a lot of money you won't fall in love with the next partner who has a gap between his front teeth.

Often, in the early stages of courtship, there need be no reason to end the relationship other than, "You don't seem like my type. You don't seem right for me." Later on in the courtship, there may be reasons aplenty for going, but chances are they have already been thoroughly talked out. When you make a decision to end it, it's important to do it in a way that you will feel good about later. You'll probably feel better if you can end it in such a way that the other person won't hate you.

Rejecting with Compassion does not guarantee that your ex-friend will take it well in the short run. Rejecting with Compassion makes it much more likely that your ex-friend will eventually remember you as a kind and honest person, and that you will think of yourself as a kind and honest person.

Compassionate rejections must be honest. At times like this, dishonesty, lies of omission, and half-truths are very hard to conceal.

Compassionate rejections have the following characteristics. They:

- don't blame the other person

- allow the other person dignity

- leave the other person with hope

- acknowledge the good experiences you have shared

- acknowledge the irrationality and unpredictability of romantic feelings in new relationships

- acknowledge your responsibility for your choices

People often tell me, "I don't know what to say." If your friend does demand to know why he does not please you sufficiently, it's okay to say, "I don't know. Love's mysterious." It's a good idea to withhold commentary on acne scars and fashion sense at times like these, and it's also compassionate.

In the later stages of courtship, things get dicier and rejections take longer, as they should. Because the two partners have invested more time and care, they need to be more cautious about the possibility that they are throwing away a good thing. Still, once it becomes clear the relationship has no future, the compassionate thing to do is to end it.

A reasonably compassionate closing statement might go something like this: "I did say that I love you, but I never promised to love, honor, and cherish 'til death do us part. I was never ready to marry you, and now my feelings have changed. I haven't lied to you. I haven't broken any promises. There's no good guy and no bad guy here. Let's leave it at that."

It might be good practice to review how you have rejected partners in the past. In some cases you might have done it more compassionately, which might have produced a better outcome. In the same way, it might be helpful to review how compassionately previous partners have rejected you. The following chart will facilitate these reflections:

Partner's name	How I rejected (or got rejected)	More compassionate scenario

Tolerating Rejection

Many people take it for granted that rejection by a potential romantic partner is about the worst thing that can happen. This is an unfortunate misconception. Fishermen have good days and bad days. They know that if they keep fishing, they will eventually catch fish. They don't take it personally. Salesmen appreciate quick rejections. It saves them time, which they can devote to their next prospect.

I am not naive. I understand that, for some people, rejection is profoundly disturbing. Still, the principles of Compassion, Attention, and Gratitude can make it less so.

The principle of Compassion might help you acknowledge that the other person is not obligated to please you. If the other person seems woefully misguided, you can wish him well despite his apparent trajectory toward unhappiness.

The principle of Attention might help you acknowledge that some things just happen, and can never be fully explained. They can only be experienced. The two of you seemed perfect for each other, but she didn't agree. Or she agreed for awhile, then inexplicably changed her mind. This was not bad or good.

It was a phenomenon of nature like a freak thunderstorm on a sunny day. If you are prejudiced against thunderstorms, you might be unhappy. If you let thunderstorms be thunderstorms, you might feel better. Don't see it as a rejection. See it as a "failure of rapport." Rapport requires equal participation from two people.

For use in cases of emergency, employ Compassion, Attention, and Gratitude to prepare new habits of thought about rejection by a possible or actual romantic partner. I'll provide one example of each, and you do the rest.

Habits of Thought Regarding Rejection

Old habit	New habit
I must lack charm or magnetism or something. No one goes for me.	I have had my fair share of love and sex, maybe more than my fair share, and I'm grateful for it. (Gratitude)
It was going so well and then I messed it up. I was trying so hard to please him, but I just couldn't do it.	This is all about style and taste and timing. There is no right or wrong here, no good or bad. I liked him more than he liked me. That happens to everybody. (Attention)
She's probably selfish. She probably wants to marry some rich guy, or someone stupid with big muscles and a nice tan. How could she do this to me?	I acknowledge her right to choose a partner who seems suitable to her. I wish her well. (Compassion)

In almost every rejection, somewhere, there is cause for Gratitude. One obvious cause for Gratitude is that many of the partners who have rejected you would not have turned out to be suitable partners. Beyond this, consider the failed romantic relationships you have experienced so far. These might have included:

- fun outings

- good laughs

- moments of joy

- new understanding about romance, love, and sex

- yummy hugs and kisses

- great sex

- new friends and acquaintances

- new understanding of the opposite sex

- new knowledge and experience regarding love, romance, and sex

People often think these things don't count if they are in the past and the relationship ended badly. This is a trap to be avoided for two reasons. First, these experiences probably changed you for the better. You became wiser and more mature and deepened your understanding of life. Even the pain prepared you for more lasting relationships in the future. Second, past experiences like these are not merely memories or reminiscences. They are the stuff your life is made of. They are the stuff *you* are made of. When you approach death and all of your good days are behind you, they still count as much as ever and perhaps more than ever. The same is true when you are still young and healthy, though it's harder to understand because your attention is more often fixed on the future.

These things are easy enough to understand. However, as always, the benefit comes not from understanding but from actually exercising the principle of Gratitude. Even the most painful or tedious failed relationships yield useful lessons and pleasurable memories worthy of Gratitude. Spend a few minutes exercising your capacity for Gratitude by recollecting such gratitude items and recording them here.

Finding the Gas Pedal

After my first date with my wife, I said to her on the way home, "We don't seem very comfortable together. I probably won't be calling you again."

She replied, "Oh, I like you well enough. I'm just nervous." Later on, we both found the gas pedal.

Many sophisticated unpartnered people assume that romantic interest either blossoms or it doesn't. One hears talk of love at first sight, chemistry, or physical attraction. Usually, people involved in courtship think and act as if mutual attraction is either totally haphazard or purely a reaction to physical attractiveness. Romantic interest is indeed partly mysterious. Nevertheless, habits of thinking can make a difference in several ways. Bad first impressions can be reversed later on. Rapport can fail on the first and second date, then blossom on the third. One-sided interest can become mutual. These things don't happen with every new partner by any means, but it is reasonable to allow some opportunities for them to occur. If you have spent enough time and energy to identify a possible new partner, make contact, and arrange a first date, it makes sense to hold on to your investment until it becomes quite clear that mutual interest and affection will not develop.

Handling Rejection with Compassion

During the time of uncertainty, consider the various ways that the principles of Compassion, Attention, and Gratitude might support the development of romantic interest in spite of a poor beginning.

As you'll recall from chapter 5, the principle of Compassion is founded upon the understanding that all people want approximately the same things for approximately the same reasons. In particular, we all desire various forms of wealth, status, and love. Mutual understanding of this principle, or even one-sided understanding, can serve as a foundation for rapport. You can put this understanding to work in the following way. Instead of trying to fathom your new friend's peculiar taste for music and odd opinions about the daily news, try to answer the following questions:

- What forms of status does she desire?

- How do these desires compare with mine?

- How does she hope to obtain status?

- What forms of love does she value most? (Possible examples include friendship, romantic passion, sexual love, close ties with family, emotional support, conventional marriage, and so on.)

- What are her occupational and financial hopes and plans? How do they coincide with my own?

These considerations might result in forthright and personal conversation, which is often a good first step in the direction of romantic interest. It's also a good way of identifying hopelessly unsuitable partners. If your date hopes to meet a nice girl who will support his drug habit, you'll know what to do.

The following example combines the experiences of several of my clients who tried out the above suggestions.

The first date didn't go too well. She dances very well and I'm pretty clumsy. I like to tell colorful jokes, which she finds vulgar. She likes word games such as crossword puzzles. I don't enjoy them. I like chess; she's never played it. We agreed we weren't hitting it off, but neither of us was exactly grossed out, either. We decided to try again. We both admitted we were interested in dating other people. On the second date, we saw a love story at the movies. Afterward, we got to talking about our previous relationships, especially what experiences made us happy and what didn't. We agreed that we both like a lot of affection, and we don't like sex without real affection. We both agreed that we want to spend our lives working hard for the sake of comfort and security, and hope to find partners who will feel the same way. We both agreed that we don't want to feel pressure from our partners to be witty, charming, or sophisticated. Pretty soon, we were holding hands. I asked her if she liked holding hands with me. She said she did, but she didn't want to be pressured for sex right away. Then she remembered that we had already talked about that. Pretty soon, we started to feel comfortable with each other. I thought about kissing her, but decided to wait. Maybe this will work out.

Handling Rejection with Attention

Many of life's most satisfying experiences involve acquired tastes. Few people like Greek olives the first time they taste them. The final result of too many hasty value judgments will be a dull and colorless life. It's the same way in dating. Many happy couples seem like odd matches. She's tall and he's short; she's got a college degree while he's a high school dropout; she's a jock while he's a poet; and so on. The principle of Attention reminds us to dispense with unnecessary value judgments.

Consider some of the unnecessary value judgments you might be most inclined to make when dating a new partner who does not exactly meet your usual specifications. In the following chart, I've summarized a few of Alathea's unnecessary value judgments with her new dating partners. After you get the idea, add some of your own.

Usual value judgments	Discussion	Possible new habits of thinking
Not tall enough.	I usually go for tall guys. No particular reason. Just a habit, I guess.	As long as he isn't freakishly short, I'm game.
Not in banking, finance, real estate, or accounting.	This is normally the kind of guy I date, but I might have better luck if I try something new.	Okay, anybody but drug dealers and panhandlers. My dad was a mortician, after all. He and my mom were very happy.
Not suave. Doesn't know what to say to wine stewards.	Once again, I guess this is just what I'm used to. Come to think of it, I prefer beer anyway.	Suave but shallow. I've been there. I'm ready to be pleasantly surprised.

Handling Rejection with Gratitude

If there is one secret to making friends and influencing people, it probably lies in treating people so that *you* will like *them*, without much concern for whether they will like you. This old aphorism suggests that practicing Gratitude for the subtle, ambiguous pleasures brought to you by new courtship partners might pay off in unexpected ways.

Let's say your blind date, Thelma, seems to offer very few opportunities for Gratitude. Frankly, she appears plain and dull. Instead of reacting in a stereotyped, predictable way, you take a few minutes to meditate on subtle possibilities for Gratitude you might have overlooked at first. After prolonged meditation, it occurs to you she smells nice. Agreed, it's a small thing, but it's a start, and you are going to spend the evening together one way or another in any case. So then you meditate on her good smell. If everything else flops, you might always remember Thelma as the girl who smelled really nice. For lack of any other handy topic for conversation, you say, "Gee, you really smell nice." Because your statement, lame as it may be, clearly comes from the heart, Thelma responds warmly. Her warmth is infectious, and you warm up too. As you warm up, Thelma seems a little less plain. An eminent historian told me this is how Anthony and Cleopatra got started.

Most Gratitude does involve unexpected and subtle pleasures. Accordingly, it's hard to plan for. Try this instead. Each time you go out with a new (or newish) partner, make mental notes on subtle qualities you notice in your partner for which you can feel genuine Gratitude, regardless of whether you feel your partner promises connubial bliss. Use the blank lines on the following page to keep a record.

Once again, Alathea offers a few of her own items (in reaction to several dates with different men) to get you started. Alathea wrote,

> *Gratitude Item*
>
> *Nice voice. Pleasant and melodious. I never really noticed how nice some voices can be.*
>
> *I liked the way he kissed me goodnight. Not grabby. Not nervous. Not proprietary. More like I am his favorite sister, and kissing me is the most natural thing in the world. It made me want to kiss some more.*
>
> *I suggested the restaurant. It might have been the world's worst restaurant. Probably new management. He noticed the food was terrible and the service worse, but he said it wasn't important and he really meant it. He said the good part was having a chance to get to know me without interruptions. That was very flattering.*

If you love someone, his ordinary features look beautiful. His ordinary mannerisms seem amusing and clever. Many of the unmarried, lonely people I know are pleasant, decent, and fun people who would make a great partner for somebody equally lonely. These people don't look like they just stepped off a magazine cover. Few of them are rich. They will excite the people who fall in love with them. To others, they will seem quite ordinary. If you need to learn to step on the gas, you might end up feeling this way about someone who will be a great partner for you.

Gratitude Item

_____

_____

_____

_____

_____

_____

Stepping on the Brake

Most people recognize that courtship should occur in a sequence of steps, and most people agree on what the ideal schedule is. First you need to meet each other, exchange phone numbers, make a date, and then, if the first few dates go well, you date rather casually for a month or two. If that goes well, you make a more serious effort to get to know each other. You share your biographies, meet each other's friends and families, and just hang out together. If this goes well, you start to get more cozy. You try some cuddling and kissing, visit each other's homes, maybe start to get sexual, and so on. (Leaping into bed too soon can spoil the relationship, particularly if you aren't sure how much you care for each other, but if you date casually for months without getting more intimate, there might be a problem.) If you feel comfortable getting cozy, you start considering a more committed relationship. After several months or more, you might feel that you are earnestly falling in love, and you might want to share the good news with your friends and families. If you are having sex, you might agree to a monogamous arrangement, or start considering the possibility of a more serious commitment to each other.

Most happy marriages have in fact followed this sequence of steps on something like this timetable. On the other hand, many couples skip or drastically shorten some of these steps. Doing so doesn't necessarily doom the relationship, but disaster is the most common result.

I know a couple who met in a hotel bar on a blind date. They drank together for a few hours, had dinner in the bar, got a room upstairs, and spent the weekend in bed. The following Monday morning before work she moved into his apartment. They married not long after and soon had children. Now it seems doubtful that they were a good match in the first place. They are in a mess. Don't do this to yourself.

Sadly, when couples skip the usual timetable for forming committed relationships, they *know* they are behaving unwisely. The problem is not stupidity or self-destruction. The problem is that they feel themselves falling in love too fast and don't know what to do. Often, one or both partners actually thinks, *Oh, boy, here I go. I'm doing it again. I'll probably regret it, but I can't stop myself.* These people *want* to step on the brake but they can't find the brake pedal.

Falling in love too quickly with unsuitable partners is a serious and complex problem that often produces painful, prolonged consequences. No simple answer will be completely satisfactory. Still, it is very helpful to understand the problem in terms of habitual beliefs. The left-hand column in the table below lists the most common habitual beliefs associated with this problem. The other two columns provide guidelines for using Compassion, Attention, and Gratitude to reduce the harm often done by these difficult habits of thought and associated painful feelings.

Problem Habit of Thought	Corrective Principle	New Habit of Thought
I am not desirable to other partners. This one may be my last chance.	Gratitude	Although I am not perfect, I have many good qualities for which I am grateful, and which other people will recognize from time to time.
Without romantic love, my life is hardly worth living.	Attention	My life is not a problem to be solved. It is not a nightmare from which only love and sex can wake me. My life is an experience to be savored.
I must spend all my time with my partner so she won't have a chance to get involved with someone else.	Compassion	I am not the only person who needs love and companionship. So does my partner, and many other people. If I relax, and trust my partner and others, I'll likely get my fair share of love in the long run.

Time spent away from my partner seems wasted.	Gratitude	Wherever I go, whatever I do, whether I am with my partner or away from him, there are good things in my life to be enjoyed.
When I'm away from my partner I'm so nervous I can't stand it.	Attention	If I face my fears calmly and patiently without regret or apology, they will gradually fade away.
Passionate romantic and sexual feelings are the only good feelings I seem capable of having.	Compassion	There are many ways to enjoy people, and many people whose company I can enjoy. Sex and romance are important forms of enjoyment, but not the only forms. There are many people in the world I can enjoy and admire.

Use this blank chart to record how your own habits of thought pull you too fast into dubious relationships. Record how you might use the principles of Compassion, Attention, and Gratitude to formulate more pleasant and constructive habits of thought when faced with these difficult feelings.

Problem Habit of Thought	Corrective Principle	New Habit of Thought

C, A, and G remind us that sex and romantic love are not necessary for happiness, nor do they guarantee happiness. In fact, obsession with the desire for sex and romantic love can get in the way of enjoying life. Still, most people enjoy romantic love and sex and would rather have it than not have it. If you are not satisfied with your love life, don't hesitate to get involved in courtship. Remembering that sex and love are not necessary for happiness will help you relax. The most important single thing to remember is to enjoy the process. If you are doing it in a way you don't enjoy, step back and rethink. The principles of Compassion, Attention, and Gratitude will help you enjoy both courtship and the love and sex that arises from it.

菜の花や
月は東に日は西に

蕪村

17

This Is the Fun Part

Although some of us are temperamentally more earnest or ambitious than others, we all want life to be fun. We will all feel disappointed and discouraged if life hasn't been fun lately. We will all feel quite depressed if we believe that the future holds no more fun for us. I don't mean only frivolous fun or comical fun. I also mean the kind of fun Woody Allen had in mind when his character in the film *Annie Hall* remarks after a great lovemaking session with someone he adores, "That was the most fun I ever had without laughing." How can we characterize this kind of fun more exactly? I don't know—the English language seems inadequate for the task.

In my opinion, a day spent at home washing the dishes and listening to the radio at the kitchen sink, lived with Compassion, Attention, and Gratitude, is more fun than a week at Disneyland, lived with resentment, unnecessary value judgments, disappointment, and envy.

A very satisfying kind of fun occurs when we unexpectedly discover the small, subtle mysteries and joys in the world around us, in its people and other living things, its events, its music and poetry and art, and in its beauties. The diligent practice of Compassion, Attention, and Gratitude makes that kind of fun happen again and again.

In previous chapters you learned about Compassion, Attention, and Gratitude partly by instruction, partly by example, and partly by practicing in challenging situations. That isn't the end of it; it's the beginning. Compassion, Attention, and Gratitude, when used wisely and diligently, enhance the quality of life in innumerable circumstances, good and bad. Compassion, Attention, and Gratitude can ease the pain caused by misfortunes. They can deepen and enrich ordinary experience for just about anyone. By now you know I don't expect you to take my word for this. By now, you may have found it out for yourself.

Of course it would be impossible to describe how to practice the three principles in every possible situation. From this point on, it's up to you to discover how to apply these three principles in response to different forms of stress and in your particular circumstances of life. That will be part of the fun, too. Chances are, you now understand Compassion, Attention, and Gratitude well enough to do that. Because you don't need to hurry, you can spend the rest of your life learning, at whatever pace is comfortable for you.

Naturally you will sometimes forget and relearn. You might become disenchanted with Compassion, Attention, and Gratitude for periods of weeks, months, or years, only to rediscover their value later on. This kind of rediscovery will deepen understanding.

Life often seems deadly serious, literally. In a way, the grim, perpetual struggle for wealth, status, and love is a symbolic attempt to deny one's mortality. Yet death does win, and when it does, the wealth and status you have accumulated are erased completely, with the exception that you can pass some of the wealth along to the next generation. Whether the love is erased by death depends partly on the kind of love you have created and shared and partly on your religious beliefs. Most people instinctively feel that the compassionate love you have shared has some kind of transcendent quality that endures after death. The love that has primarily involved mutual favors, mutual admiration, and other self-serving purposes seems less eternal.

In *Buddhism Without Beliefs,* author Stephen Batchelor encourages his readers to reflect deeply upon this question: "Given that death is inevitable, and the time of death uncertain, how shall I live?"

I answer Batchelor's question this way:

- I will live each encounter, each task, and each experience as if it really matters. This way, in my subjective experience, each encounter, task, and experience actually begins to really matter. Whether they really matter in the scientific or practical sense is irrelevant. Whether they really matter to anyone else is not necessarily important. All I ask is that they take on a sense of enduring significance for me, so that I am sustained by this felt significance during times of hardship, nourished by it during times of hard work, and cheered by it at all times.

- I will live each encounter, each task, and each experience as if time does not exist. I will live as if each moment lived in Compassion, Attention, and Gratitude has no beginning and no end. Again, it is absurd to ask whether this is objectively true. All I ask is to feel its truth frequently, in a way that cheers and sustains me.

Spend a few minutes reflecting, praying, or meditating on the same question: Given that death is certain, and the time of death uncertain, how shall I live? Record your answers here:

_____

_____

_____

_____

_____

In the rest of this chapter, I'll suggest some tools and tricks you can employ to refresh your understanding of Compassion, Attention, and Gratitude. With luck, some of these will help you remember insights and techniques you would otherwise forget or become complacent about. Some will stimulate your ingenuity when you need to practice the principles in new and challenging situations.

Exercises

Life Experiences Regarding Compassion

Certain personal experiences have enhanced your capacity for Compassion. For instance, someone you love and admire might have taught you a lesson in Compassion. Perhaps you independently discovered the principle of Compassion at some time, or enjoyed a powerful insight about it. You might also recall times when the principle of Compassion would have been especially helpful if only you had understood it. These incidents might have occurred quite recently, in your earliest childhood, or anywhere in between. Recalling and reflecting upon these experiences might help you practice Compassion more effectively.

Date	Who was involved?	What happened?	Reflections

Life Experiences Regarding Attention

As with Compassion, certain personal experiences might have enhanced your capacity for Attention. Recalling and reflecting upon these experiences may help you practice Attention more effectively.

Date	Who was involved?	What happened?	Reflections

Life Experiences Regarding Gratitude

As with Compassion and Attention, certain personal experiences have enhanced your capacity for Gratitude. Recalling and reflecting upon these experiences may help you practice Gratitude more effectively in the future.

Date	Who was there?	What happened?	Reflections

C, A, and G Heroes

No one ever practices C, A, and G perfectly, all the time. Some people, however, consistently practice one or more of these three principles in a way that is both inspiring and instructive. The person may be contemporary, historical, or fictional. When you encounter such people, keep a record to deepen and perpetuate the instruction and inspiration.

Person's name	How does this person embody C, A, or G?	Reflections

Running for the Love of the Race

Running for the love of the race is different from striving for "more." It may be goal-directed activity, but the activity is generally within the boundaries of Compassion, Attention, and Gratitude. Consequently, it is likely to benefit the quality of your life and also the quality of life for the people around you. It's a good idea to notice when you are running for the love of the race, and to reflect upon these times. This chart can be a record of past or present times when you have done that. Be specific. Record particular incidents. Make a note of when and where it was, and what you were doing. Then record further reflections.

Date	What I was doing	Reflections

Compassion Game Worksheet

This is a challenging exercise you can try alone or with a partner. Choose some person you know or know of for whom you can feel no Compassion. He or she can be contemporary, historical, or fictional. Ask yourself, *How could I think compassionately about this person?* Follow the usual steps for compassion. First ask yourself, *Is it true that she wants about the same things as me, for about the same reasons? Is it true that she gets about the same good feelings as me when her desires are gratified, and that she gets about the same bad feelings as me when her desires are thwarted? Is it true that the main ways we differ are in our circumstances and the methods we employ for getting what we want?* Try to think of ways that these things are true. See if a genuine feeling of Compassion develops for the person in question.

Where and when:

Person in question:

In what ways is it true that he/she desires about the same things as me?

In what ways is it true that he/she feels about the same good and bad feelings as me?

New feelings of Compassion that develop from this exercise:

Compassion Log

Sometimes when you are specifically practicing Compassion, you will have an important experience you will want to remember and reflect upon. Record such experiences here.

Date	The incident	Reflections

Attention Log

Sometimes when you are specifically practicing Attention, you will have an important experience you will want to remember and reflect upon. Record these important experiences here.

Date	The incident	Reflections

Gratitude Log

Sometimes when you are specifically practicing Gratitude, you will have an important experience you will want to remember and reflect upon. Record such experiences here.

Date	The incident	Reflections

Un-Compassion Log

There will of course be times when you think, act, or speak in a manner not at all compassionate. Later on, you might realize what happened. It is worthwhile to reflect upon these incidents.

Date	Who	What happened; what was said?	Reflections

Un-Attention Log

There will of course be times when you think, act, or speak in a manner not at all consistent with the principle of Attention. Later on, you might realize what happened. It is worthwhile to reflect upon these incidents.

Date	Who	What happened; what was said?	Reflections

Un-Gratitude Log

There will of course be times when you think, act, or speak in a manner not at all consistent with the principle of Gratitude. Later on, you might realize what happened. It is worthwhile to reflect upon these incidents.

Date	Describe the experience	Reflections

Epiphanies

Epiphanies are moments when the veil of illusions is suddenly lifted. At those times, the world is perceived with particular clarity as beautiful, perfect, and just as it needs to be. This is your treasure box of epiphanies. For each event, record where and when it occurred, what you were doing that might have evoked it, and any notes that might help you remember it or understand it more deeply. Use additional sheets as necessary.

Where and when	What I was doing	Description

Good Things I Can Happily Get Along Without

Henry David Thoreau said, "That man is richest whose pleasures are cheapest."

The tempting item	Tantalizing daydreams regarding the tempting item	How life could be lovely without the tantalizing item

Dream Journal

Certain dreams may instruct you, warn you, or inspire you regarding the practice of Compassion, Attention, and/or Gratitude. Record these dreams and reflect upon them.

Date	Describe the dream	Reflections

Gratitude Inkblot

When you're having trouble with Gratitude in a challenging situation, recall the analogy of the inkblot. Presented with the same inkblot, some people see ugly things, others see interesting or beautiful things. They are all there. They are all real. Think of a challenging situation as an inkblot and look for other ways to perceive it that might not have occurred to you. Don't force yourself. Just open up your imagination. You may discover opportunities for Gratitude.

Where and when	The challenging situation	Other ways of perceiving the challenging situation (circle the ones that really make sense)

Senseless Acts of Random Kindness—Yours—Present

Senseless acts of random kindness are a kind of sacrament to the three principles of Compassion, Attention, and Gratitude. Remember that you do them for your own benefit, not for anyone else's. If and when you commit such acts, record them briefly here. By recalling them later and reflecting upon them, you may emphasize benefits you receive by doing them.

Where and when	What happened?	Reflections

Senseless Acts of Random Kindness—Yours—Past

The senseless acts of random kindness you have committed in the past may represent some of the most important acts you have committed in your life up until this point. Do your best to remember them and briefly document them. Record your reflections.

Where and when	What happened?	Reflections

Senseless Acts of Random Kindness—Heroes

You may learn of senseless acts of random kindness committed by other people. These incidents may inspire or instruct you. Use this sheet to record and reflect upon such events.

Where and when	What happened?	Reflections

Attention Worksheet

This worksheet will help you organize your thoughts when you're attempting to practice Attention in a challenging situation.

Where and when:

_____

Describe challenging situation:

_____

Your nonattentive thoughts (unnecessary value judgments):

_____

_____

Your nonattentive actions:

_____

What do you fear will happen if you are more attentive in this situation?

_____

Possible new thoughts for this situation, consistent with Attention:

_____

_____

Which of the above thoughts can I live with comfortably?

_____

How do my feelings change when I substitute new attentive thoughts in place of the old nonattentive ones?

_____

_____

Is there some way that I could behave more attentively in this situation?

_____

Gratitude Worksheet

This worksheet will help you organize your thoughts when you're attempting to practice Gratitude in a challenging situation.

Where and when:

_____

Describe challenging situation:

_____

Your nongrateful thoughts:

_____

_____

Possible alternative grateful thoughts (brainstorming):

_____

_____

Which of the possible grateful thoughts can I actually accept comfortably?

_____

_____

How do my feelings change when I substitute new grateful thoughts in the place of the previous nongrateful ones?

_____

_____

Does smiling warm up the feeling of Gratitude?

_____

Is there something I can do or say to encourage or endorse grateful feelings that may have arisen? What happens if I do that?

_____

Don't wait for the fun part. *This* is the fun part.

Epilogue

菜の花や
月は東に日は西に

蕪村

Living according to the principles of Compassion, Attention, and Gratitude does not require any particular opinion regarding current affairs, environmental protection, or religious dogma. It does not require you to lay down in front of every bulldozer to protect every endangered subspecies of garter snake. It does not require you to boycott every product that might have been made by oppressed workers. Actually, living according to the principles of Compassion, Attention, and Gratitude doesn't require you to do anything at all. Living according to the three principles is a choice you must make freely and because you value the quality of your own life. But you might find in the end that there are practical advantages to maintaining your personal integrity, working for peace and justice, and developing greater concern for people you don't know and other life forms that aren't cute or don't directly serve mankind's needs.

Compassion, Attention, and Gratitude are personal choices to which individuals commit themselves because it feels right to them to do so. If there are certain social or environmental issues dear to you (or even if you haven't quite made up your mind yet where you stand) I urge you to think about what the three principles mean to you, and use that information to develop your own moral guidelines to live by. I did exactly that in my first book, *How to Want What You Have*, which lists ten moral suggestions that I developed based on the three principles. By contrasting "suggestions" with "commandments," I intended some gentle self-mockery. I am not a Moses-like figure, and of course I do not converse with the Supreme Being. My ten moral suggestions, which I try to live by in daily life, arise logically from the principles of Compassion, Attention, and Gratitude, and I have found them useful as guidelines in my dealings with the world. I hope your own moral principles will be useful to you as well.

Stop for a moment and think about everything in this book that made sense to you. Think about the things you learned about yourself while doing the exercises, and take into account everything you know about Compassion, Attention, and Gratitude. Then, in the blank spaces below, write your list. You don't *need* to come up with ten, of course. The items can be as general as "Show more Compassion toward animals," if you like.

_____

_____

_____

_____

_____

_____

_____

_____

How do you hope to live your life differently in accordance with these guidelines? Look at your list again and for each of the guidelines you listed, reflect on how your past and present way of life accords with that particular item. You may find it useful to return to this list every few months (or years) to see how your behavior and outlook have changed. Hopefully, you'll be well on the road toward wanting what you have!

菜の花や
月は東に日は西に

蕪村

Further Reading

Batchelor, Stephen. *Buddhism Without Beliefs: A Contemporary Guide to Awakening*. New York: Putnam, 1997.

Beck, Aaron, et al., *Cognitive Therapy of Depression*. New York: Guilford, 1979.

Burns, David D. *Feeling Good: The New Mood Therapy*. New York: Avon, 1980.

Csikszentmihalyi, Mihaly. *Flow: The Psychology of Optimal Experience*. New York: HarperCollins, 1990.

Dass, Ram, and Paul Gorman. *How Can I Help?* New York: Alfred A. Knopf, 1985.

Forster, E. M. *Howard's End*. New York: Knopf, 1991.

———. *A Room With a View*. New York: Knopf, 1993.

Galsworthy, John. *The Forsyte Saga*. New York: Scribner, 1932.

Huxley, Aldous. *The Perennial Philosophy*. New York: HarperCollins, 1970.

Kabat-Zinn, Jon. *Wherever You Go, There You Are*. New York: Hyperion, 1994.

Lebell, Sharon. *Epictetus: The Art of Living*. New York: HarperCollins, 1995.

Marcus Aurelius and His Times. Roslyn, N.Y.: Walter J. Black, 1945.

Miller, Timothy. *How to Want What You Have: Discovering the Magic and Grandeur of Ordinary Existence.* New York: Henry Holt, 1995.

Nhat Hanh, Thich. *Peace Is Every Step.* New York: Bantam, 1991.

Seligman, Martin. *Learned Optimism.* New York: A. A. Knopf, 1991.

The Way of Life According to Lao Tzu. New York: Capricorn Books, 1944.

Trollope, Anthony. *The Warden.* New York: Oxford University Press, 1998.

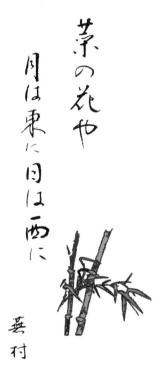

Timothy Miller, Ph.D., invites you to send him copies of completed worksheets that might instruct or inspire other students of Compassion, Attention, and Gratitude. By submitting them, you consent to possible future publication. Neither your name nor other identifying details will be divulged to anyone, nor will your name and address be provided to any mailing list or advertiser. Anonymous submissions are equally welcome.

Timothy Miller hopes to publish an occasional low-cost or no-cost newsletter for interested students of Compassion, Attention, and Gratitude. Please feel free to submit your name and address. Your privacy will be protected completely.

Send worksheets or newsletter addresses to:

Tim Miller
P.O. Box 147
Lodi, CA 95241

If you have an e-mail address, you can subscribe to an automated e-mail list (sometimes known as a "listserve" or "listserver") which allows students of Compassion, Attention, and Gratitude to converse, encourage, support, and inspire each other by means of an ongoing electronic conversation indexed by subject. Once again, your e-mail address will not be divulged to anyone without your explicit consent.

To learn how to subscribe to the e-mail list or to obtain other information about it, send an e-mail message to:

wantwhat@serenity.org

In the body of your message, type: **info wantwhat**

Some Other New Harbinger Self-Help Titles

High on Stress: A Woman's Guide to Optimizing the Stress in Her Life, $13.95
Infidelity: A Survival Guide, $13.95
Stop Walking on Eggshells, $14.95
Consumer's Guide to Psychiatric Drugs, $13.95
The Fibromyalgia Advocate: Getting the Support You Need to Cope with Fibromyalgia and Myofascial Pain, $18.95
Healing Fear: New Approaches to Overcoming Anxiety, $16.95
Working Anger: Preventing and Resolving Conflict on the Job, $12.95
Sex Smart: How Your Childhood Shaped Your Sexual Life and What to Do About It, $14.95
You Can Free Yourself From Alcohol & Drugs, $13.95
Amongst Ourselves: A Self-Help Guide to Living with Dissociative Identity Disorder, $14.95
Healthy Living with Diabetes, $13.95
Dr. Carl Robinson's Basic Baby Care, $10.95
Better Boundaries: Owning and Treasuring Your Life, $13.95
Goodbye Good Girl, $12.95
Being, Belonging, Doing, $10.95
Thoughts & Feelings, Second Edition, $18.95
Depression: How It Happens, How It's Healed, $14.95
Trust After Trauma, $13.95
The Chemotherapy & Radiation Survival Guide, Second Edition, $14.95
Heart Therapy, $13.95
Surviving Childhood Cancer, $12.95
The Headache & Neck Pain Workbook, $14.95
Perimenopause, $13.95
The Self-Forgiveness Handbook, $12.95
A Woman's Guide to Overcoming Sexual Fear and Pain, $14.95
Mind Over Malignancy, $12.95
Treating Panic Disorder and Agoraphobia, $44.95
Scarred Soul, $13.95
The Angry Heart, $14.95
Don't Take It Personally, $12.95
Becoming a Wise Parent For Your Grown Child, $12.95
Clear Your Past, Change Your Future, $13.95
Preparing for Surgery, $17.95
The Power of Two, $12.95
It's Not OK Anymore, $13.95
The Daily Relaxer, $12.95
The Body Image Workbook, $17.95
Living with ADD, $17.95
Taking the Anxiety Out of Taking Tests, $12.95
Five Weeks to Healing Stress: The Wellness Option, $17.95
Why Children Misbehave and What to Do About It, $14.95
When Anger Hurts Your Kids, $12.95
The Addiction Workbook, $17.95
The Chronic Pain Control Workbook, Second Edition, $17.95
Fibromyalgia & Chronic Myofascial Pain Syndrome, $19.95
Flying Without Fear, $13.95
Kid Cooperation: How to Stop Yelling, Nagging & Pleading and Get Kids to Cooperate, $13.95
The Stop Smoking Workbook: Your Guide to Healthy Quitting, $17.95
Conquering Carpal Tunnel Syndrome and Other Repetitive Strain Injuries, $17.95
An End to Panic: Breakthrough Techniques for Overcoming Panic Disorder, Second Edition, $18.95
Letting Go of Anger: The 10 Most Common Anger Styles and What to Do About Them, $12.95
Messages: The Communication Skills Workbook, Second Edition, $13.95
Coping With Chronic Fatigue Syndrome: Nine Things You Can Do, $13.95
The Anxiety & Phobia Workbook, Second Edition, $18.95
The Relaxation & Stress Reduction Workbook, Fourth Edition, $17.95
Living Without Depression & Manic Depression: A Workbook for Maintaining Mood Stability, $17.95
Coping With Schizophrenia: A Guide For Families, $15.95
Visualization for Change, Second Edition, $15.95
Postpartum Survival Guide, $13.95
Angry All the Time: An Emergency Guide to Anger Control, $12.95
Couple Skills: Making Your Relationship Work, $13.95
Self-Esteem, Second Edition, $13.95
I Can't Get Over It, A Handbook for Trauma Survivors, Second Edition, $16.95
Dying of Embarrassment: Help for Social Anxiety and Social Phobia, $13.95
The Depression Workbook: Living With Depression and Manic Depression, $17.95
Men & Grief: A Guide for Men Surviving the Death of a Loved One, $14.95
When Once Is Not Enough: Help for Obsessive Compulsives, $13.95
Beyond Grief: A Guide for Recovering from the Death of a Loved One, $13.95
Hypnosis for Change: A Manual of Proven Techniques, Third Edition, $15.95
When Anger Hurts, $13.95